www.wadsworth.com

wadsworth.com is the World Wide Web site for Wadsworth and is your direct source to dozens of online resources.

At *wadsworth.com* you can find out about supplements, demonstration software, and student resources. You can also send email to many of our authors and preview new publications and exciting new technologies.

wadsworth.com
Changing the way the world learns®

CORRECTIONAL LEADERSHIP

A CULTURAL PERSPECTIVE

Stan Stojkovic

University of Wisconsin, Milwaukee

Mary Ann Farkas

Marquette University

THOMSON

WADSWORTH™

Australia • Canada • Mexico • Singapore • Spain • United Kingdom • United States

THOMSON
WADSWORTH

Senior Executive Editor, Criminal Justice:
  Sabra Horne
Assistant Editor: *Dawn Mesa*
Editorial Assistant: *Paul Massicotte*
Marketing Manager: *Dory Schaeffer*
Marketing Assistant: *Neena Chandra*
Signing Representative: *Jan Holloway*
Project Manager, Editorial Production:
  Emily Smith
Print/Media Buyer: *Jessica Reed*

Permissions Editor: *Stephanie Keough-Hedges*
Production Service: *Buuji, Inc.*
Text Designer: *Adriane Bosworth*
Copy Editor: *Linda Ireland, Buuji, Inc.*
Cover Designer: *Yvo Riezebos*
Cover Image: *Corbis Images*
Compositor: *Buuji, Inc.*
Text and Cover Printer: *Phoenix Color
  Corporation*

For more information about our products,
contact us at:
**Thomson Learning Academic
Resource Center
1-800-423-0563**
For permission to use material from this text,
contact us by:
Phone: 1-800-730-2214   **Fax**: 1-800-730-2215
Web: http://www.thomsonrights.com

Library of Congress Control Number:
  2001012345

ISBN 0-534-57429-7

Wadsworth/Thomson Learning
10 Davis Drive
Belmont, CA 94002-3098
USA

Asia
Thomson Learning
5 Shenton Way #01-01
UIC Building
Singapore 068808

Australia
Nelson Thomson Learning
102 Dodds Street
South Melbourne, Victoria 3205
Australia

Canada
Nelson Thomson Learning
1120 Birchmount Road
Toronto, Ontario M1K 5G4
Canada

Europe/Middle East/Africa
Thomson Learning
High Holborn House
50/51 Bedford Row
London WC1R 4LR
United Kingdom

Latin America
Thomson Learning
Seneca, 53
Colonia Polanco
11560 Mexico D.F.
Mexico

Spain
Paraninfo Thomson Learning
Calle/Magallanes, 25
28015 Madrid, Spain

We dedicate this book to those correctional professionals who on a daily basis exhibit effective correctional leadership practices and behaviors.

BRIEF CONTENTS

CONTENTS

PREFACE

As we enter the 21st century, the world of corrections is rapidly changing. Correctional institutions, for example, now house over 1.5 million people. If we include local institutions of confinement, such as jails, the total population under correctional authority well surpasses 2 million people. The demands and expectations placed on prison leaders, managers, and administrators are daunting: Many correctional institutions are overcrowded, lack adequate program space, operate beyond their budgetary capabilities, and are having difficulty recruiting and maintaining their workforce. Correctional leaders also have other demands placed on them by legislatures, courts, and public interest groups. In an unprecedented call, traditional correctional administrators and managers are being asked to do more than *manage;* they are being asked to *lead* their organizations out of the difficulties they face.

Correctional leaders face much uncertainty. There is no formal role with a title of "correctional leader" within prisons, as there is for managers and administrators. For many, the term is unsettling and confusing. However, the *behaviors* of correctional leaders resonate within correctional institutions. Our view is that correctional leadership behavior exists everywhere in the prison hierarchy. Whether exhibited by correctional officers or the prison warden, correctional leadership behaviors are what engender effective prison operations. Our central purpose in this book is to convey the dynamics of correctional leadership as behaviors that perpetuate and enhance organizational culture.

ORGANIZATION OF THE BOOK

This first edition of *Correctional Leadership: A Cultural Perspective* presents an alternative way of thinking about correctional organizations and how they are led. The book brings organizational culture to the fore and underscores the role of managers as *leaders* who influence and shape this culture. Culture is understood as an *amalgam of relationships with organizational members,* and leadership is conceptualized as *identifying, developing, nurturing, and maintaining* these relationships. The correctional organization is comprised of multiple cultures existing at different levels along the organizational hierarchy. Leaders are faced with the challenge of uniting employees across these competing cultures in a common mission and purpose. We acknowledge the vital role of leadership in identifying a commonality of values, ideas, and concerns and in transmitting and transforming culture.

Chapter 1 introduces the concepts of leadership and organizational culture. Most importantly, a link is made between effective correctional leadership and organizational culture. We hold the view that correctional leaders are the primary individuals who influence and shape the culture of their organization. It is their responsibility to transmit a vision, formulate mission statements, identify goals, articulate objectives, and assign tasks *in collaboration* with their employees. Effective leaders know how to work with people, how to motivate and challenge, and how to define values and exemplify desired behavior. The centrality of leadership to the development of a positive culture within the prison is underscored.

The historical and theoretical development of key perspectives and theories of organization, management, and leadership is explored in Chapter 2. The significance and application of these theories in the correctional organization and for correctional management is the focal point. The chapter works toward the development of an integrative approach to understanding organizational culture and subcultures within a prison and the influential aspects of leadership in relation to that culture. We provide a useful framework by which to view organizational culture and, specifically, the culture of corrections.

In the early prison literature, the culture of correctional work was perceived as a unitary subculture of guards with rigid, procustodial values and anti-inmate, antiadministration attitudes. The major drawback of this view was that guards were considered to be an "undifferentiated mass" incapable of alternative behavior and individual thought, and administrators were thought to be incapable of changing or influencing this entrenched culture. The prison culture has also been described as fragmented, as being composed of several predominant types of correctional officers. Although this view recognizes individual variation among organizational members, it neglects the cohesive aspects of the culture and offers administrators little hope of coalescing these varied attitudes and beliefs. Finally, the prison culture has been portrayed as three distinct cultures: the "higher-ups," middle management, and line officers. This conceptualization creates barriers among cultures and does not recognize the commonality of goals and concerns. Chapter 3 uses these models of culture as a springboard to develop a more comprehensive theoretical framework of correctional culture. An integrated theory is presented in which each level of the organization is perceived as *multicultural* and interactive with the other organizational levels, as well as with the external environment.

In Chapter 4, the multiple layers of the correctional culture and the differentiation within this culture are explored. The cultures are systematically analyzed and described in several different ways, ranging from the very tangible overt manifestations that one can see and feel to the deeply embedded, unconscious basic assumptions of organizational members. Bureaucratic characteristics, strong militaristic overtones, the fortified physical architecture, and the values of custody and control are the overt manifestations of the formal or official culture of corrections. Organizational members' underlying values and beliefs about their jobs and about how their tasks should be carried out, assumptions about prisoners and about their coworkers and supervisors, and focal concerns such as the danger and unpredictability of correctional work, constitute the informal culture.

The cultural orientations of correctional administrators are the focus of Chapter 5. The various dimensions of culture as expressed by administrators at different levels (e.g., middle-level management versus top-level management) are framed by the work setting and the tasks these administrators perform. The different focal concerns held by these administrators with regard to correctional leadership, and how these concerns affect organizational culture, are at the heart of the chapter. Moreover, the chapter discusses how external influences, including governors, legislators, employee unions, the courts, and members of the media, profoundly affect how correctional leaders perform their jobs. Correctional leaders must learn to work with, and cultivate, these various interest groups in order to accomplish their mission.

The purpose of Chapter 6 is to present ideas on how correctional culture can be transmitted and, in some cases, transformed. Once the mission statement is identified and correctional values are agreed upon, it is the responsibility of correctional leaders to transmit these ideas to employees. In some cases, this means transforming the culture so that ways of doing business are altered and made more consistent with the values and approaches specified by those in leadership and management positions. A particular emphasis in this chapter is on strategies to coalesce differing interests and individuals in the correctional environment into one congruent work group. Discussion focuses on the potential benefits to correctional administrators of such an effort, as well as the limitations and difficulties associated with such an initiative.

The final chapter of the book presents the primary issues facing corrections and the major strategies that should be considered by correctional leaders in the new millennium. The authors conclude with informed speculation on the challenges that correctional leaders in prison organizations will face in the future. Organizational culture will continue to be an important construct for both correctional leaders and society. The future of correctional leadership rests with how well it confronts the complexities associated with the organizational culture. The chapter also discusses possible future directions for both research and policy development concerning correctional leadership and organizational culture.

We have included case scenarios at the end of each chapter. The scenarios are designed to allow the reader to apply the organizational theories and concepts learned to specific prison situations and interactions. We hope these scenarios will stimulate critical thought regarding the complexities of prison work and the role that leaders can play in influencing, inspiring, and changing organizational culture.

In addition, we encourage students and instructors to visit Wadsworth Thomson Learning's criminal justice resource Web site at: http://wadsworth.com /criminaljustice_d. This site provides valuable information regarding this book as well as other resources in the criminal justice field.

ACKNOWLEDGMENTS

We have many people to thank for the creation of this book. We would like to express our gratitude and sincere appreciation to Ms. Sabra Horne at Wadsworth Thomson Learning. She assisted us in many ways with the production of this book. Without her continued support we would never have been able to finish the book. In addition, we would like to express our appreciation to the many reviewers who critically examined the chapters as they were being produced and provided valuable feedback. Their valuable insights contributed significantly to the final product. A special thanks is also extended to Ms. Linda Ireland for her competent and careful editing of this book.

We are also indebted to a number of correctional professionals with whom we have worked over the past 10 years as consultants. They are too great in number to mention individually here, but we want to especially thank the California Department of Corrections and its Leadership Institute for providing us with access to many truly dedicated and hard-working correctional administrators. Without their insights and assistance, many of the ideas in this book would never have been developed.

Finally, we want to thank our friends and families for providing encouragement and support. Dr. Rick Lovell provided a keen eye and analytical perspective in helping us to understand correctional leadership. We also appreciate the help of Drs. David Kalinich and Mark Pogrebin, fellow consultants with the California Department of Corrections' Leadership Institute. And we thank our families: Ilija and Milan Stojkovic; Jeff, David, Gabor, and Tom Farkas; and Ron, Elana, and Hannah Rose Rubin. These friends and families gave us the foundation to produce this book. They provided the support, but we produced the chapters. Therefore, we accept full responsibility for the content presented.

Stan Stojkovic

Mary Ann Farkas

REVIEWERS

Terry Baumer, *Indiana University—Purdue University, Indianapolis*

Bruce Bikle, *California State University, Sacramento*

Tom Dempsey, *Christopher Newport University*

M. George Eichenberg, *Wayne State College*

Tara Gray, *New Mexico State University*

David Horton, *St. Edward's University*

Betty Wright Kreisel, *Central Missouri State University*

Jess Maghan, *University of Illinois at Chicago*

James Marquart, *Sam Houston State University*

David Olson, *Grand Valley State University*

James D. Stinchcomb, *National Institute for Paralegal Arts and Sciences*

Jeanne B. Stinchcomb, *Florida Atlantic University*

Thomas Franklin Waters, *Northern Arizona University*

Harold Williamson, *University of Louisiana, Monroe*

CORRECTIONAL LEADERSHIP AND ORGANIZATIONAL CULTURE

CORRECTIONAL LEADERSHIP AND ORGANIZATIONAL CULTURE

According to the Bureau of Justice Statistics (2000), the total number of persons under correctional supervision falls just short of 6 million. Of these 6 million offenders, roughly 1.2 million are housed in correctional settings. These offenders are placed in various types of institutions, including, but not limited to, minimum security camps, medium security correctional institutions, and maximum security prisons. In total, there are approximately 1,500 correctional institutions in the United States, all guided by state and federal statutes and administrative regulations. Oversight for these institutions involves the efforts of correctional leaders, managers, officers, and other assorted correctional staff.

Correctional leaders and managers are responsible for directing the efforts of correctional staff toward the accomplishment of specific goals. The goals of correctional institutions, however, are multiple and conflicting. Although we expect correctional leaders and managers to maintain a secure and safe environment for staff and inmates, increasingly we are expecting correctional institutions to do more than this. Research has documented how many persons within the public expect prisons to not only punish offenders but also provide some services to offenders, so that their chances of exhibiting law-abiding behaviors on release will be better than they were before they went to prison (Applegate, Cullen, & Fisher, 1997).

For correctional leaders and managers, the expectations of the various publics and specific interests prove to be challenging. More than ever before, correctional leaders and managers face multiple expectations and infinite demands on their limited time and finite resources. Correctional leaders and managers are told to "do more with less." We live in a period in which the very essence of what government service actually entails is coming under question, particularly in correctional work.

In addition, the operations of correctional systems are being challenged. Private companies are establishing themselves as a major force in the corrections field. More and more states are contracting with private companies to handle overflow offenders who cannot be housed in traditional public institutions. Serious questions have been raised concerning the proper role of these private entrepreneurs in the corrections field (Shichor, 1997). Moreover, important questions are being raised about *how* correctional work is accomplished. Correctional leaders and managers are at the forefront of this discussion. Yet, an analysis and examination of correctional work from the perspective of correctional leaders and managers has been lacking (Fernandez, 1998).

Some interesting works have begun to address correctional leadership and management over the past couple of decades, most notably the work of DiIulio (1987) and Wright (1994). Both of these writers stressed the importance of management and leadership to correctional institutions. Where they differed was in *what* they considered necessary for effective leadership and management. For DiIulio, effective prison management meant a "tight ship," with an emphasis on order, amenity, and service as the primary goals of an institution. For Wright, however, prison leadership meant being both "tight but loose" in the managing of a prison. Wright focused on the people processes that define correctional work. For him, similar to DiIulio, effective prison leadership meant control, but the realization of control was a product of an interplay among staff and inmates, one predicated on team building and shared vision.

Neither DiIulio nor Wright, however, expanded on their original analyses to further explain *how* correctional leaders and managers actually lead or manage. Each author accentuated the importance of control to prisons and even suggested methods or behaviors that make prison control more possible, but their works contain very little discussion about organizational culture and how prison control is influenced to such a great degree by that culture. There has been no detailed examination of the connection between prison leadership and management and organizational culture.

We believe that through effective leadership and management, a positive organizational culture is engendered, and that through this culture, prison goals are realized. In subsequent pages and chapters, we offer a nexus between *prison leadership* and *prison culture*. Our central thesis is that for prisons to be effective places, they must be both managed and led by competent people who are cognizant of the fact that at the core of correctional work is the *art of developing, nurturing, and maintaining relationships*. Effective correctional leaders are those persons who know how to work with people, both staff and offenders, in such a way that a positive *culture* is developed. A positive culture is a product of effective management and leadership.

LEADERSHIP AND CORRECTIONS

The purpose of this book is to examine correctional leadership and the role of leaders in the development of correctional culture. Correctional leaders play a pivotal role in the development of a specific culture within their organizations, but there has been a lack of attention paid to the importance of leadership to organizational culture and the operations of correctional institutions. Instead, much of the existing literature on leadership focuses too much on management. Notwithstanding the comments of some writers who believe that the distinction between management and leadership in corrections is artificial (Carlson, 1999), we believe that, given the current conditions most correctional administrators face, more attention needs to be paid to leadership issues than to management concerns.

This is not to minimize the importance of vigilant management practices to correctional institutions. If correctional leaders are to be effective in their institutions, they must be attentive to the day-to-day operations, yet this is not enough. Correctional leadership today involves the participation of leaders at many different levels. The functioning of the prison is important, but equally important is the degree to which correctional leaders are, for example, responsive to the political processes that affect their institutions. In fact, we argue later that many correctional leaders are woefully ignorant of how to function within the political arena, and as a result of this ignorance, their institutions suffer.

Many correctional administrators have learned how to manage, but know very little about leadership. They are versed in a myriad of strategies on how to *manage* their employees. Like other public managers, they have been told the importance of total quality management (TQM), management by objectives (MBO), and how to be a 10-minute manager, yet they have very little knowledge of how to *lead* their institutions. They may be able to respond to a court order, for example, but too often they are unaware of how they got into a situation that resulted in court involvement. Responding to court orders is the appropriate role of a manager, but a leader will also analyze policies, procedures, and practices and question how these reflect the organization's values. Such questioning is the basis upon which leadership is, in part, predicated.

In this book we present leadership ideas that move beyond the concerns of correctional managers. We suggest that effective leadership is proactive in nature; consists of vision, values, and mission; and, most importantly, comprehends that the leader is the person to whom correctional employees look for guidance and direction. The most effective correctional leaders have set the example for their organizations to create a highly particularized and unique culture. Whether it was Warden Ragen in Illinois, George Beto in Texas, or Richard McGee in California, what made these leaders giants in the correctional field is that they had definitive ideas on how prisons should be run, and they also *led* the way.

The most effective correctional administrators have been leaders who had visions that they carried out as they fostered unique cultures among their employees. Ragen ran the Stateville prison with an iron fist and every employee knew it (Jacobs, 1977). Beto employed "building tenders" to control large prison populations in Texas, something that later became controversial and illegal, but he was able to transmit a culture that made the Texas Department of Corrections a model for the rest of the country (Marquart & Crouch, 1989). McGee truly believed in the term *corrections*; he viewed the central purpose of corrections to be the effective change and betterment of prisoners (Glaser, 1995).

Each of these correctional leaders of the past had a vision and mission for his prison, and they all understood the importance of the role they played in transmitting culture. They knew they had to set the moral tone for their prisons, and each one of them valued his employees. They set examples and worked with subordinates in such a way that an identifiable culture became discernible in each of their prisons. The cultures of these correctional systems became distinctive and were traced back to the behaviors of these leaders. Over time, these leaders' names became synonymous with corrections in their states. One could not think about corrections in Illinois, Texas, or California without mentioning their names. Even in these states today, the names of these leaders are almost mythical, and folklore has developed to continue the transmission of the cultures they helped to create.

Current correctional leaders would benefit from a careful reading of the stories of these pivotal figures in correctional history, as well as others such as Carlson at the federal level and Wainwright in Florida. Such an examination reveals how these leaders understood the importance of leadership behavior to the functioning of their institutions. Moreover, a primary theme within much of this history is the fact that effective correctional leadership entails the creation of a specific culture that reinforces the values of both leaders and employees.

Ragen in Illinois was an astute politician who could manipulate political figures and anyone else who affected the prison. He led the Stateville prison with a high degree of forcefulness and promoted respect among correctional staff to such a degree that his style became the defining element of Illinois prison culture. In Texas, Beto encouraged correctional staff to follow rules and existing methods of doing business through his infamous style of walking around the institution, sometimes unannounced to employees. He reinforced a culture among his employees where there was a right way to run prisons, and for the most part, he received respect and admiration from them. Similarly, McGee in California used his connections and knowledge of politics to get prisons built in the southern part of the state and to advance the interests of correctional employees. He was one of the first heads of a department of corrections to use scientific knowledge and empirical evidence as a basis for making correctional policy. He supported and promoted a culture where knowledge and the scientific method were important to correctional decision making (Glaser, 1995).

For all these correctional leaders, the creation and support of a culture was extremely important. They understood that if correctional leadership was to be effective, attention had to be paid to instilling specific values among employees, and the most promising way to achieve this objective was through the development of a culture that was consistent with their own ideas and values on how correctional organizations were to be run. It is to this topic that the efforts of this book are directed. We, too, believe that the central tasks of correctional leadership are related to engendering a correctional culture.

A correctional culture is directed by those at the top of the organization. The true test of a correctional leader's effectiveness is how well he or she instills a culture that is consistent with the needs of employees and the demands of the various and conflicting publics, as well as sensitive to the political realities of the environment in which correctional leaders function. This is no small order, but by paying attention to organizational culture, correctional leaders can both address the pressing concerns of the day and be more responsive to the vagaries of citizens and political leaders.

LEADERSHIP DEFINED

The literature on leadership is fairly expansive. Definitions of leadership have been offered, examined, and analyzed for many decades (see Stojkovic, Kalinich, & Klofas, 1998, for a review of this literature). Systematic examinations of leadership have produced a hodgepodge of definitions and axioms, all of which are both valid and questionable at the same time. Nevertheless, for the purposes of this book, we argue that *leadership is fundamentally a process by which an organizational culture is engendered such that tasks, objectives, and goals are achieved through the coordinated efforts of supervisors and subordinates.* This definition of leadership is predicated on the principle that leaders have the primary responsibility for developing relationships among correctional personnel such that a successful organizational culture is possible.

The literature on correctional leadership and management has failed to identify the importance of culture to prisons. Hence, much of what has been offered to prison administrators in the way of prescriptive information lacks an awareness of the connection between leadership and culture. In fact, at one level, leadership and culture can be understood as inseparable, since you cannot think of leadership without comprehending the impact the leadership has on institutional culture. Effective correctional leadership involves a process whereby leaders both influence and are influenced by culture. This view is most vividly expressed by Edgar Schein (1997) when he states: "Neither culture nor leadership, when one examines each closely, can really be understood by itself. In fact, one could argue that the only thing of real importance that leaders do is to create and manage culture and that the unique talent of leaders is their ability to understand and work with culture" (p. 5). The remainder of this book is devoted to explaining the nexus between correctional leadership and correctional culture.

DEFINING ORGANIZATIONAL CULTURE

The definition of organizational culture is problematic. (Chapter 2 provides a review of the theoretical models of understanding culture.) For some, organizational culture refers to a patterned way of responding to the work environment and its multiple tasks. For others, it refers to the accepted ways in which language is used and shared among supervisors and subordinates. Organizational culture reflects multiple meanings within organizations.

We adopt the ideas expressed by Schein (1997, pp. 8–10) that organizational culture can be understood on multiple levels within a work setting based on the following dimensions: observed behavioral regularities, group norms, espoused values, formal philosophy, rules of the game, climate, embedded skills, habits of thinking, shared meanings, and root metaphor. Schein (1997, p. 12) suggests that at its core, organizational culture is "a pattern of shared basic assumptions" that people follow in organizations to perform tasks, solve organizational problems, and arrive at consensus concerning the direction of the organization. This is where the nexus between organizational culture and leadership is formed. Leaders either forge organizational culture, or they are forged by it.

A basic premise of this book is that *the perpetuation of a specific organizational culture is the domain of leadership.* Correctional leaders are responsible for formulating mission statements, identifying goals, articulating objectives, and assigning tasks. In addition, these processes are not done in an organizational vacuum but, instead, through *collaboration* with employees. In short, organizational purpose is defined through group collaboration.

In this way, leaders not only direct but are also influenced and directed by organizational culture. Leaders, however, have more of a direct voice in the perpetuation of culture, since they determine the organizational *set* or *tone* for employees to follow. We agree with Schein (1997, p. 15) that if leaders do not comprehend the importance of organizational culture, it will define them. The creation of a specific organizational culture becomes the central task of leadership. If organizational culture is not *directed* by leaders, then a void is created. This void, in many instances, is filled by the most vociferous voices within the organization. Such is the case in many correctional organizations.

Most importantly, we need to discuss how correctional culture affects the world of the prison on two dimensions: the *organizational level* and the *individual level*. At the organizational level, processes and practices determine organizational outcomes. In simple language, we want to know how organizational culture shapes where the prison organization is moving and how well it accomplishes tasks, achieves objectives, attains goals, and pursues its mission. At the individual level, we want to know how culture affects employees. Is there, for example, a relationship between organizational culture and employee satisfaction, performance, and retention? Answers to these questions are of primary concern for both correctional leaders and managers. In fact, one could argue that addressing these concerns is what leadership and management are all about.

Later chapters address how leadership and management have differing *perspectives* on concerns at the organizational and individual levels; both viewpoints are critical to the creation and maintenance of organizational culture. Leaders and managers are inextricably intertwined in organizations, and in correctional organizations their individual roles in shaping culture cannot be overstated.

LEADERSHIP AND ORGANIZATIONAL CULTURE: THE NEXUS

Correctional leadership is critical to the creation of a specific organizational culture. To a large degree, correctional leaders get what they engender in their prison settings. There is a phrase in business circles that you never get what you deserve, only what you negotiate. Similarly, correctional leaders get what they negotiate with their managers and subordinates, and other interested parties such as governors and legislative bodies (Riveland, 1997). The primary responsibility for the development of specific cultural norms resides with correctional leaders. Too often correctional leaders and correctional managers have abdicated their responsibility to lead and manage their organizations. In some respects, DiIulio (1987, p. 3) is correct when he states that traditional explanations of prison management are inadequate and do not place the responsibility for running prisons in the correct place. The responsibility belongs to correctional leaders and managers.

This is not to suggest, however, that total responsibility lies with correctional leaders and managers. Such leaders and managers have very little say concerning crime rates, legislative commitment to fund corrections appropriately, and, to some degree, the quality of personnel they hire (Breed, 1998). Nevertheless, correctional leaders can *influence* these processes as part of an effective leadership strategy. They can do everything in their power to propose rational ideas concerning crime control, some of which would include correctional efforts and some of which would not; they can work with legislators and others to affect the quantity and quality of resources they receive; and they can be more quality-conscious about who they hire and how they train subordinates for corrections work. We would be remiss, however, if we believed improved correctional leadership is the ultimate panacea to correctional problems.

Our position is that correctional leaders and correctional managers are crucial to the functioning of prisons, but they can only do so much. Corrections is highly influenced by economics, politics (discussed more in later chapters), and the expectations of citizens concerning the purposes and goals of prisons. We can only expect correctional leaders to define and operationalize what the English philosopher David Hume referred to as the "moral sense" in their organizations. This moral sense is developed through the values, beliefs, and norms the correctional leader believes are the most critical to the operations of the prison. The correctional leader, through these values, beliefs, and norms, sets the stage for the type of organizational culture he or she wants to transmit.

Leadership and organizational culture function in a recursive fashion, affecting each other in ways that are not always discernible. It is clear that correctional leaders are critical to the functioning of prisons. In addition, correctional managers are important to prisons, but correctional leaders and correctional managers are not the same people. Each has distinctive roles and responsibilities. Too often correctional leaders have fallen into the trap of being caught up in the day-to-day minutia of running their institutions, to the detriment of their leadership roles. Schein (1997) suggests the fundamental difference between leaders and manager as follows:

> If one wishes to distinguish leadership from management or administration, one can argue that leaders create and change cultures, while managers and administrators live with them. (p. 5)

For correctional leaders, this distinction is profound. The capable correctional leader works toward the creation of a culture that is consistent with his or her values concerning optimal correctional performance. Correctional leaders define the parameters of behavior and performance that are acceptable for subordinates within the prison; correctional managers work within these parameters by developing appropriate policies and procedures, assisting correctional staff toward the completion of their tasks, and evaluating whether organizational objectives and goals are being met.

For prisons to be effective places, both correctional leaders and correctional managers are needed (Phillips & McConnell, 1996). There are many successful correctional leaders and correctional managers, yet the latter far outnumber the former. A good correctional manager is not necessarily a good correctional leader. Working within prison parameters is one thing; creating those parameters is another matter. The field of corrections has come a long way in the development of correctional managers, yet very little has been done to develop correctional leaders. Both correctional practitioners and those who study prisons can see that very little has been done to expose correctional managers to new ideas, to impress upon them the importance of vision to correctional leadership, or to help them find ways to break out of traditional paradigms concerning prison operations (Stojkovic, Kalinich, Lovell, Pogrebin, Corley, & Roberts, 1997).

Such a dearth of views has made many correctional departments unable to address the fundamental issues and concerns that shape and influence their present operations as well as their future conditions. One of the most pressing issues facing correctional leaders is the role of politics in their departments. For many correctional leaders, *politics* is a dirty word, yet the recognition of the political nature of correctional leadership is essential. How well a correctional leader plays the political game defines not only his or her tenure but also the degree to which he or she is able to influence organizational culture.

As a result, correctional leadership, politics, and organizational culture are inextricably intertwined. The effective correctional leader understands that politics is played on many dimensions both internal and external to the prison. Internally, the political in-fighting among competing employee and management groups is constant. Whether it be correctional unions fighting with management over labor issues, or female employees feeling unappreciated and unrecognized by the department of corrections, politics is the daily fodder that all correctional employees confront. At the external level, politics means dealing with significant stakeholders and powerful lobbies that have a direct impact on correctional budgets and operations.

It is at the level of external politics that traditionally correctional leaders have acted similar to managers. Being very well versed on what their prisons need, correctional managers have been effective in expressing these concerns to legislators, governors, and notable political interests. Yet, they have not been effective in garnering long-term political support for their institutions and in developing political coalitions that will address correctional issues beyond the immediate budgetary horizon (Baro, 1988). Due, in large part, to a lack of correctional vision, correctional leaders have been forced to focus on the immediacy of the moment and have lost sight of the importance of strategic planning and visionary leadership in expressing their concerns and ideas for their prisons over a longer time frame. A form of correctional myopia has prevented them from being able to respond to both short-term threats from their environment and long-term issues concerning the direction their prisons are taking.

To be effective, correctional leaders must become, in part, politicians. As a correctional leader stated to one of the authors of this text, "Corrections has always been political; it is just *more* political today" (emphasis added). Correctional leaders must develop and hone political skills to be successful in the 21st century. Political skills require more attention to stakeholders, the creation of vision for both departments of corrections and those who lead prisons, and awareness that corrections has been and will continue to be part of a political process.

The politics of the 21st century focus on how finite resources should be appropriated across the infinite demands of many special interest groups.

Corrections is just one competitor for these finite resources. Correctional leadership will have to be at the forefront of developing political skills and marshaling political resources if the visions of correctional leaders are to be realized. Correctional leaders will have to carry their visions to both subordinates and external constituents. They will have to engender successful political coalitions and a specific organizational culture that recognizes the importance of managers and employees to their mission. In this way, correctional leadership, politics, and organizational culture will be pivotal to the direction in which corrections heads during the 21st century.

LEADERSHIP AND CORRECTIONS: CONCLUDING COMMENTS

Our intention in writing this book has been to reveal what we believe is a useful and exciting way to view correctional leadership. Like authors of similar works in the police field (Crank, 1998), we believe it is the right time to examine correctional leadership in the context of organizational culture. The connection between correctional leadership and organizational culture is apparent to many correctional practitioners. The importance of correctional leadership in the development and maintenance of an organizational culture cannot be overstated. The future of correctional leadership rests with how well it confronts the complexities associated with organizational culture.

Correctional leaders are the *primary* individuals who influence the organizational culture within prisons. Documentation and investigation of organizational culture should be a central activity for those interested in the prison. In this way, the academic researcher and the correctional professional are connected in their quest to improve prisons. For the researcher, investigations into the relationship between correctional leadership and organizational culture may reveal interesting theoretical insights into the operations of prisons. For the correctional practitioner, particularly correctional leaders and managers, such an investigation should yield useful and practical information on how employees and prisons can be better led and managed.

The focus of this book is not on management, although this is not to devalue the importance of management to correctional institutions. It is clear that effective management skills are necessary for correctional institutions to function. There has been, however, an overabundance of discussion concerning management issues in the literature and among correctional professionals. The topic of correctional management has been adequately addressed in recent works such as *The Effective Corrections Manager* (Phillips and McConnell, 1996); *Prison and Jail Administration: Practice and Theory* (Carlson and Garrett, 1999); *Correctional Management: Functions, Skills, and Systems* (Houston, 1999); and *Quick Reference to Correctional Administration* (Phillips and Roberts, 2000). These works, along with others, have stressed the importance of management to correctional institutions, but their examination of leadership has been limited and circumscribed. We need works that distinguish and note the important differences between leaders and managers in the corrections field.

Borrowing from Bennis (1989), we can offer the following distinctions between correctional managers and correctional leaders:

CORRECTIONAL MANAGERS	CORRECTIONAL LEADERS
Operate within a structure	Deal with people in a structure
Are concerned with control	Inspire trust and involvement among employees
Live in the short-term	Adopt a long-term perspective
Ask how and when	Ask what and why
Keep their eyes on the bottom line	Keep their eyes on the horizon
Imitate	Originate
Accept the status quo	Challenge the status quo
Are good soldiers	Are their own persons

Effective prison administrators understand these distinctions and see the utility in having both good managers and capable leaders. Due to many factors in recent correctional history, however, the trend in contemporary correctional institutions has been to accentuate management concerns over a leadership focus. With greater court-ordered bureaucracy, tighter legislative control and scrutiny, and more direct involvement by governors, correctional institutions have been led by managers.

For example, the current boom in prison construction is, in part, a function of the leadership void in corrections. Few have stood up to say that it is wrong to build so many prisons or to confront the effect such massive construction has had on the quality of prison life for both staff and inmates, as well as on society in general. The result has been a near-anomic state in prisons, in which correctional managers and employees have been left with no direction, resulting in a diminished and fragmented correctional culture. Moreover, this has occurred while other major dimensions of correctional culture have been changing: greater racial and sexual integration of the workplace, an increase in staff lawsuits against prisons, and proliferation of unionization of the workforce. It is for these reasons that correctional leadership is so critical to prison organizations.

The challenges facing correctional leaders are daunting, and the core of correctional leadership in the 21st century will be based on how well leaders mold and shape their organizational cultures to address these pressing concerns. In the words of James Gomez, the former director of the California Department of Corrections, corrections will need "more leaders, not just managers, to face the challenges of the [21st] century." We hope the analyses in the subsequent chapters will shed some light on why correctional leadership is so important to prisons and, most importantly, why influencing correctional culture will be the central task of correctional leaders in the 21st century.

In the next chapter we examine various theoretical models concerning culture in general and their connection to correctional organizational systems and leadership. The purpose is to offer a theoretical foundation for investigating leadership and organizational culture. We also propose an integrative model of organizational culture and show its linkage to leadership. Subsequent chapters address the larger organizational culture of corrections, a specific exploration of correctional officer subcultures, the culture of correctional administrators, how correctional culture can be transmitted and transformed by correctional leaders, and the future of correctional leadership in the 21st century.

CASE SCENARIO   *What Is a Prison Leader?*

Deputy Warden Patrick Ford knew his day in front of the corrections subcommittee of the legislature was going to be tough, but he didn't realize how difficult things were going to be until legislators started asking questions about the recent charges of brutality that were being levied against his warden and some correctional officers at the prison. He knew he had to face the heat, since the warden had recently announced his retirement and was not going to cooperate with the subcommittee. Many of the questions directed at Ford were related to what one legislator referred to as the "cover your ass" mentality that has permeated the prison's culture for decades.

From the beginning, Deputy Warden Ford tried to place a positive spin on the situation. When asked by one legislator who really ran the prison, the warden and his staff or corrupt correctional officers, Ford responded by saying that a majority of correctional officers at the prison were good employees who took their jobs seriously and were not corrupt or brutal in their treatment of prisoners. To this response, another legislator asked, "If that is true, Mr. Ford, then why do we have a scandal every couple of years at the prison involving officers doing the wrong thing? Four years ago it was drug smuggling by officers. This year it is brutality by officers. What is going on at the prison where these types of problems are occurring over and over again?"

Deputy Warden Ford tried to restate his earlier position that most correctional staff are good people trying to do a difficult job. To this answer, the legislator retorted, "Mr. Ford, your answer is not good enough and doesn't explain the systematic problems that the prison has had for many years. Isn't it true that the retiring war-

den preferred to be kept in the dark concerning the activities at the prison and even condoned violence against inmates and supported a code of silence as a mechanism to cover the illegal and improper acts of some correctional officers?" Ford responded that some management personnel wished the warden would have been more involved in what was going on at the prison. He also added that all officers are given formalized training on how to perform their jobs and are held accountable to specific performance standards. Angrily, the legislator stated, "Mr. Ford, I am not talking about how you count prisoners, or what dressing is on the dinner salads for inmates, or even how many hours of training correctional officers receive. I am talking about ethics and doing the right thing. You can document all you want about how much training officers receive and what their performance assessments indicate, but none of that will really address the problems that I want to talk about concerning the prison and what needs to be done."

"I don't know what else to tell you, sir," responded Ford, to which the legislator replied, "And isn't that the problem, Mr. Ford? You want to talk like a manager, and I want you to talk like a leader." Deputy Warden Ford wondered whether the distinction offered by the legislator made any sense.

Case Scenario Questions

1. How else could Deputy Warden Ford have prepared for the meeting with the legislative subcommittee? Should he have known many of the questions and concerns of the legislators in advance?

Case Scenario continued

2. What is the difference, if any, between isolated negative incidents, for example, correctional officer corruption or brutality, and more systematic problems among correctional staff? Are these problems in any way related to the culture of the prison, and if so, how can leaders influence such a culture?

3. Is there a difference between a correctional manager and a correctional leader? If so, what are the differences? Is the legislator's distinction in the case scenario relevant to prison organizations?

REFERENCES

Applegate, B. K., Cullen, F. T., & Fisher, B. B. (1997). Public support for correctional treatment: The continuing appeal of the rehabilitative ideal. *The Prison Journal, 77,* 237–258.

Baro, A. (1988). The loss of local control over prison administration. *Justice Quarterly, 5,* 3.

Bennis, W. (1989). *On becoming a leader.* Reading, MA: Addison-Wesley.

Breed, A. F. (1998). Corrections: A victim of situational ethics. *Crime and Delinquency, 44*(1), 9–18.

Bureau of Justice Statistics (2000). *Prison and jail inmates midyear 1999.* Washington, DC: U.S. Department of Justice.

Carlson, P. M. (1999). Management accountability. In P. M. Carlson & J. S. Garrett, *Prison and jail administration: Practice and theory* (pp. 41–46). Gaithersburg, MD: Aspen.

Carlson, P. M. & Garrett, J. S. (1999). *Prison and jail administration: Practice and theory.* Gaithersburg, MD: Aspen.

Crank, J. (1998). *Understanding police culture.* Cincinnati, OH: Anderson.

DiIulio, J. J. (1987). *Governing prisons: A comparative study of correctional management.* New York: Free Press.

Fernandez, M. (1998). *A review of the literature on leadership: Implications for future correctional research.* Paper presented at the annual meeting of the Academy of Criminal Justice Sciences, Albuquerque, New Mexico, March 1998.

Glaser, D. (1995). *Preparing convicts for law-abiding lives: The pioneering penology of Richard A. McGee.* Albany, NY: State University of New York Press.

Houston, J. (1999). *Correctional management: Functions, skills, and systems* (2nd ed.). Chicago: Nelson-Hall.

Jacobs, J. (1977). *Stateville: The penitentiary in mass society.* Chicago: University of Chicago Press.

Marquart, J., & Crouch, B. (1989). *An appeal to justice: Litigated reform of Texas prisons.* Austin, TX: University of Texas Press.

Phillips, R. L., & McConnell, C. R. (1996). *The effective corrections manager.* Gaithersburg, MD: Aspen.

Phillips, R. L., and Roberts, J. W. (2000). *Quick reference to correctional administration.* Gaithersburg, MD: Aspen.

Riveland, C. (1997). Correctional leader and public policy skills. *Corrections Management Quarterly, 1*(3), 22–25.

Schein, E. H. (1997). *Organizational culture and leadership* (2nd ed.). San Francisco: Jossey-Bass.

Shichor, D. (1997). Three strikes as a public policy: The convergence of the new penology and the McDonaldization of punishment. *Crime and Delinquency, 43*(4), 470–492.

Stojkovic, S., Kalinich, D., & Klofas, J. (1998). *Criminal justice organizations: Administration and management* (2nd ed.). Belmont, CA: West/Wadsworth.

Stojkovic, S., Kalinich, D., Lovell, R., Pogrebin, M., Corley, C., & Roberts, J. (1997, September). Correctional leadership education into the 21st century: The California Leadership Institute. *Federal Probation*, 50–54.

Wright, K. (1994). *Effective prison leadership.* Binghamton, NY: William Neil.

CULTURE: THEORETICAL AND ORGANIZATIONAL ISSUES

The importance of leadership and its relationship to culture was introduced in the previous chapter. The past few decades have seen the development of a complex and somewhat confusing body of knowledge regarding the role and functions of a manager and those of a leader. Nonetheless, we need to examine the origins of contemporary leadership perspectives in order to truly value their offering to the study of organizations and organizational culture. The theories and theorists in this chapter represent a broad array of approaches and were selected more to illustrate the diverse thought regarding organization, management, and leadership than to act as a definitive work.

Many different conceptual models for understanding organizations have been developed. Various perspectives have dominated at different historical times. Organizational theories are generally classified depending on their focus and the problem studied. They may be broadly classified into structural, behavioral, integrative, cognitive, and transformational perspectives, although other classification schemes also have been used. Examples of the structural perspective include scientific management theory, classical management theory, Weber's bureaucracy, and Barnard's leadership theory. The behavioral view consists of theories such as Mayo's Hawthorne studies, McGregor's Theory X and Theory Y, Herzberg's two-factor theory, decision theory, and Etzioni's structuralist model. The integrative view covers systems theory and contingency theory. The cognitive perspective includes symbolic organization theory. Finally, the transformational view of organizations and management consists of various strains of transformation theory.

The level of organizational analysis of the manager's role and of the leader's role is quite distinct in many of the theories. Some researchers only scratch the surface, concentrating on the manipulation by management of the process or characteristics of some formal aspect of organizational structure. Others focus on management's influence on the behavior or attributes of members within organizations. In the following sections, we examine several organizational theories and their major components. We then apply the theories to corrections to define the relevant issues and to extract those theoretical concepts that are most useful for our conceptualization of the culture of an organization and the role of leadership.

ORGANIZATIONAL AND MANAGEMENT THEORIES

Structural Perspectives

Structural perspectives addressed the structure and design of work and organizations. These theories were essentially a reaction to the period of great industrial growth in the early 1900s. The crux of these theories was that organizations could be systematically and scientifically designed and managed. The more efficient use of human beings in the production process was the concern, not the broader psychological and social aspects of human behavior in organizations. Management processes and functions were key to the scientific design. The duties and tasks of a manager were actually defined and analyzed in structural theories. Management played an integral role in the coordination and organization of activities in the workplace by directing workers to perform tasks more efficiently and productively. In this way the work efforts of employees were carefully monitored and controlled. Included in the structural perspectives are the scientific management, classical management, bureaucratic, and Barnard's leadership theories.

Scientific Management Theory. According to scientific management theory, management was just that, a science, with work activities that were precisely designed and structured. Frederick Taylor (1911) is considered the founder of scientific management theory, or "Taylorism," and the "principles of scientific management." A mechanical engineer at the Bethlehem Steel Works, Taylor observed the inefficiency of workers doing the same tasks in different ways. He sought to improve their efficiency and productivity by designing the one best way to perform each job.

Although Taylor drew attention to the more efficient use of labor through task management, he overlooked the influence of an organization's culture on a worker's motivation and resultant productivity. A workplace culture is created through the sharing of sentiments of workers and relations between organizational members. If the norms of a foundry's culture are that of "bucking the system," for instance, the laborers will produce at a minimum to comport with set norms. On the other hand, if the culture is participative and workers feel a sense of ownership, more work effort may be expended. Taylorism overemphasized mechanization and task management and ignored this human relations aspect of an organization. In addition, Taylor conceived of a manager as one who monitors and controls workers through task and time management. The ability of management to be "leaders" who inspire employees to achieve was not considered.

Scientific management is rather difficult to apply to correctional work. There are certainly tasks, such as head counts and periodic patrols of assigned areas, that can be defined, analyzed, and standardized. Yet the mechanistic movements so compatible with production in manufacturing industries are incongruent with the unpredictability and variability inherent in correctional work. Mechanistic movements require automatic and controlled responses. Correctional officers must be ever on the alert and highly observant of inmate movement and interactions. This state of alertness would be difficult to break down into simple, rhythmic tasks. There is no rhythm to correctional tasks or to an environment characterized by unpredictability. Correctional work is sometimes boring and monotonous, while at other times exciting and "adrenalin-pumping." The automatons required for "Taylorism" would not fit well in corrections.

Classical Management Theory. The work of Henri Fayol (1949) typifies the classical school of management. Fayol, who wrote at the same time as Taylor, was a French manager of an industrial and mining company. He proposed general principles of management believed to be essential to the "good working order" of an organization (see Figure 2-1). The first principle was a division of work in which the employer became specialized and skilled in the same task. Fayol

FIGURE 2-1   *Fayol's Principles of Management*

1. Division of work	8. Centralization
2. Autority and responsibility	9. Scalar chain (line of authority)
3. Discipline	10. Order (material and social)
4. Unity of command	11. Equity
5. Unity of direction	12. Stability of tenure of personnel
6. Subordination of individual interests to the general interest	13. Initiative
7. Remuneration	14. Esprit de corps

viewed authority, the right to give orders and the power to exact obedience, as another central principle of management, with responsibility being its natural consequence.

Discipline concerned obligations of "obedience, application, energy, behavior, and outward marks of respect observed in accordance with the standing agreements between the firm and its employees" (Fayol, 1949, p. 22). The principles of unity of command with work orders from one superior only and unity of direction with one head and one plan for work activities were also high managerial priorities. In addition, fair and satisfactory remuneration of employees was an important motivator to be used by management.

The scalar chain of command from the ultimate authority to the lowest ranks was necessary in order for communications to follow a defined path. The manager also needed to ensure order, which consisted of both material and social order. *Material order* meant "there must be a place appointed for each thing and each thing must be in its appointed place" (Fayol, 1949, p. 36). *Social order* was defined as an "appointed place for every employee and every employee be in his appointed place" (p. 36). Fayol believed that *equity* and *equality of treatment* also must be considered in managing employees. Effective management involved efforts to ensure the stability or retention of employees. Finally, a manager had to develop an esprit de corps or cohesion and common interests among workers for a more harmonious and more efficient work environment.

As with "Taylorism," classical management theory required the worker to be highly specialized in the same task. In corrections, this specialization of tasks is hard to identify. According to Fayol, specialization involves swiftness, skill, and accuracy in performing a single task. The variety of tasks in correctional work that require a particular skill or speed complicates the application of classical management theory. The theory was more befitting the mechanical movements of goods production than working with large numbers of human beings. Most certainly, the human service aspects of corrections cannot be quantified.

Moreover, Fayol viewed managers as those who exacted compliance with managerial objectives from their workers through the development of an esprit de corps. This would prove a challenge in a correctional environment where officers may have formed subcultures and cliques that modify formal objectives or directly oppose the officially designated goals. While Fayol proposed specific tasks for managers, he did not anticipate the spontaneity and diversity of situations in a work environment such as corrections. Furthermore, the development of cohesiveness and a shared purpose among correctional officers requires a more dynamic, involved, and inspirational leadership role than the maintenance role of Fayol's manager.

Weber's Bureaucracy. While Taylor and Fayol concentrated on efficiency and control of workers and their tasks, sociologist Max Weber (1964) was concerned with the consequences of authority structures for the organization and its members. He believed the mechanization of industry led to the development of bureaucracy, a "mechanistic" form of organization. Bureaucracy was needed for order and rationality because of technological advancement in society. It provided an ordered system of superordination and subordination with supervision and control of workers and work activities.

Weber identified the characteristics of a bureaucracy (see Figure 2-2). Hierarchical authority denoted the levels of authority in an organizational structure. Specialization with work functions differentiated by type of task and division of labor was another bureaucratic feature. A system of rules was necessary to organize the activities of employees and to govern their performance. Selection of personnel was based on their technical qualifications. The employees then had to be thoroughly and expertly trained and prepared for their tasks. The sixth characteristic of a bureaucracy, impersonal relations, guaranteed that rules and controls would be applied uniformly, avoiding a personalized approach to work matters. Weber feared the social consequences of this bureaucracy, including robotic behavior, depersonalization, and oppressive routine. He deplored the type of worker that mechanism and the routine of bureaucracy selected and formed, and the loss of human spontaneity and inventiveness.

With its rigid lines of authority and rank structure, the formal culture of corrections exemplifies the ordered system of superordination and subordination that Weber described. Nonetheless, this authority structure in corrections may not "hold up" under the strain of day-to-day operations and interactions. Line officers fashion their own culture and establish their own group norms of how best to perform their tasks within the confines of their units or cell blocks. What works in one facility or unit within a correctional institution may not be practical or effective in another. Although Weber feared bureaucracy would lead to automatons, this is not necessarily so in corrections. Bureaucracy may also lead to innovative ways to circumvent its constraints. The work of correctional officers is circumscribed by procedural guidelines and directives, but nonetheless, no programmed agenda is able to cover the myriad of situations to which officers must respond. So officers use their discretion in handling certain situations that arise and develop unique ways of handling inmates. Of necessity, they may develop a culture with differing objectives and ways of thinking than that of the formal, bureaucratic culture.

Barnard's Leadership Theory. Chester Barnard's 1938 book, *The Functions of an Executive,* was based on his experience as the president of the New Jersey

FIGURE 2-2   *Weber's Characteristics of a Bureaucracy*

1. Hierarchical authority
2. Specialization and division of labor
3. System of rules
4. Selection of personnel based on technical qualifications

5. Training
6. Impersonal relations
7. Employment viewed as career

Bell Telephone Company. Barnard believed that there were two structures in an organization, the formal and informal, oftentimes with differing objectives. These structures could be brought together into a cooperative whole through the right kind of leadership. He introduced the idea of leadership as a form of communication with workers. He defined the fundamental qualities of a leader as: vitality and endurance, decisiveness, persuasiveness, responsibility, and intellectual capacity.

Vitality and endurance constituted a compelling force or motivator for workers in the organization. Decisiveness was a propensity or willingness to make a decision and the capacity to do so. The quality of persuasiveness involved understanding the point of view, interests, and conditions of those to be persuaded. Responsibility was the development of a collective purpose morally binding on subordinates. Finally, a leader had to possess the intellectual capacity to lead. This theory realized the pivotal role of a leader in developing and sustaining a commonality of purpose. The leader coordinated social relationships into a cooperative whole.

Barnard's theory is important to an understanding of the correctional organization because of his recognition of the informal and formal components and the role of the leader in reconciling the objectives and perspectives of both. This is a complex task in corrections where multiple subcultures exist, often with contradictory objectives. It is further hampered by rank distinctions that may promote differing values. Line officers are made keenly aware of their status with the color of their uniform shirt, rank insignia, and their required deference to middle and upper management. Indeed many officers refer to their supervisors as "white shirts." Their view is essentially that white shirts neither understand the realities of correctional work nor value the perspective of line staff. They fragment into a subculture(s) with their habits of thinking and ways of doing. Barnard urges leaders to try to understand the point of view of workers in order to persuade them to the leader's objectives. The ultimate goal is a cohesive organization based on a commonality of purpose.

The Behavioral Perspective

The behavioral perspective emphasized the psychological and sociological aspects of management and the human aspects of an organization. Behavioral science research was applied to organizational theories and the practice of management. Early studies focused on the social and psychological needs of workers and a set of leadership traits or characteristics that would motivate or influence the behavior of individual workers. Later research emphasized the relational aspects of leadership, the relations between managers and employees and their effect on worker performance and attitude. The assumptions and attitudes that managers have toward their employees influence the way they interact with and treat their employees. The key to higher productivity is a managerial strategy designed to increase the motivation and job satisfaction of workers. Theories in the behavioral perspective identify the biological, psychological, and social needs of human beings and their quest for fulfillment through their work and membership in an organization. It is in these theories that we see culture emerging as a way of viewing the membership and functioning of an organization. A subculture may emerge as workers form informal groups based on their understanding of their purpose and function within the organization and based on their relationships with supervisors and coworkers.

The Hawthorne Studies. Elton Mayo (1933) asserted that the rapid pace of industrial development in the early 1900s concentrated on the scientific aspects of management and work and disregarded the social needs, participation, and interactions among employees. He has been referred to as the "father of the human relations movement" because of his focus on the importance of human behavior and interaction with others at work. Mayo's research showed the significance of groups and their influence on the behavior of the individual worker. Fatigue and monotony, and their effects upon workers, were other topics of interest to him.

Mayo is widely known for his experiment at the Hawthorne Works at the Western Electric Company. A group of workers were selected for observation of the effect of various changes, including temperature, light, and humidity, on the conditions of work. Mayo observed that employees developed a sense of participation and cooperation as their opinions were consulted (Mayo, 1946). Social relationships developed that extended to after-work hours. Results of the experiment showed a better mental attitude, an eagerness to come to work, and a greater enjoyment of the job among the workers. Mayo's research led to the recognition of what has been called the "Hawthorne effect"—that human factors influence productivity and job satisfaction.

For corrections, this recognition of the influence of the informal work culture and of social interaction among workers has interesting implications. Correctional officers basically rely on their colleagues to share the workload, cover each other's duties, and assist in inmate altercations and disputes. Although some research has concluded that there is a lack of solidarity among correctional officers, more recent research points to the importance of examining solidarity within the context of particular work groups or work situations. The degree of solidarity or cohesiveness among officers may vary by unit within a facility or an institution (Farkas, 1998). It may depend on the particular work culture. Subcultures may emerge that reflect the goals and the values of the official structure, or subcultures may appear that directly challenge the formal goals of the organization and act as a divisive force. Correctional leaders must be attuned to the relations among their workers and their workers' sentiments toward the job and the organization. Mayo might suggest that leaders solicit opinions and suggestions from line staff to develop a feeling of participation and inclusion among their employees.

Theory X and Theory Y. According to McGregor (1967), the role of management was to create conditions (an organizational environment) such that members at all levels of the organization could best achieve by directing their efforts toward the overall goals of the organization. He is perhaps best known for his Theory X and Theory Y. These theories are not managerial strategies, but rather underlying beliefs or assumptions about the nature of humans that influence managers to adopt a particular strategy. According to Theory X, most human beings have an inherent dislike of work and will avoid exerting themselves if possible. Since human beings dislike work, they must be coerced, controlled, or threatened with punishment in order to motivate them. Theory Y assumptions, on the other hand, include the belief that work is as natural as play for most people and that workers will exert effort toward goals provided they feel a commitment toward those objectives. The average person can learn to accept, even seek, responsibility.

McGregor incorporated the motivational theory of the behavioral scientist Abraham Maslow (1954) into his view of the nature of humans. Maslow theorized that human needs are organized in a hierarchy with physiological and safety needs at the lower end, and the social needs of belonging and love, esteem, and self-actualization at the higher level. Higher-order needs are satisfied internally, whereas lower-order needs (pay and tenure) are primarily satisfied externally. Only when the lower-level needs are met can humans achieve the higher-order need of self-actualization. According to Theory X, lower-order needs dominate and preoccupy people. Conversely, Theory Y holds that higher-order needs predominate and motivate individuals.

Theory X correctional administrators assume that their staff needs constant oversight and guidance in order to accomplish assigned tasks. This controlling style of management strongly influences the prison culture. Unquestioned deference to authority and strict adherence to all rules, regulations, and directives characterize the culture. Under Theory X, line officers feel compelled to blindly follow orders and rules without taking any independent action. The uncertainty and unpredictability of correctional work, however, makes this style of management difficult to implement. The Theory Y administrator has more flexibility to manage the complexity and spontaneity of correctional work. This administrator attempts to understand the group norms and shared understandings among workers, tries to involve the officers in decision making, and seeks ways to enrich employees' jobs.

Herzberg's Two-Factor Theory. The two-factor theory originated from a study by Herzberg, Mausner, and Synderman (1959). The researchers interviewed more than 200 accountants and engineers regarding positive and negative incidents in their work experience. From this data, Herzberg developed a two-factor theory of motivator and hygiene factors. Motivators or growth factors were factors such as autonomy, achievement, and advancement that were intrinsic to the job and motivated a worker to exert more effort and to perform better. Hygiene factors met physiological, security, or social needs. These extrinsic factors included pay, job security, and company policy. They satisfied the lower-order needs and prevented dissatisfaction. Herzberg believed that the primary determinants of job satisfaction and job enrichment were the intrinsic motivators, and the primary causes of job dissatisfaction were extrinsic hygiene factors.

Herzeberg's theory helps us to understand the nature of correctional work and what may enrich the job for officers. Intrinsic factors, such as the challenge of the job, satisfy higher-order needs and are the primary determinants of job satisfaction. Johnson (1996) points out that in a public culture of aloofness and social distance, many correctional officers engage in human service activities with inmates despite the time constraints, extra effort required, and disapproval of colleagues and supervisors. He concludes that this is because human service activities enrich the officer's job to become more rewarding and less stressful. In short, officers seek opportunities to be useful and to make a difference in inmates' lives. Recognition of these attitudes by correctional leaders could create a culture of participation and collaboration with employees and, ultimately, a commonality of purpose.

Decision Theory. Decision theory focused on the choices that occur before action is taken and on the processes of decision making by administrators. Herbert Simon (1947) believed that administration is equivalent to decision making. He published a book entitled *Administrative Behavior: A Study of Decision-making Processes in Administrative Organizations* in which he stressed that a general theory of administration must included principles of organization to ensure correct decision making. Setting the agenda and prioritizing organizational needs, representing the problem in a manner that generates possible solutions, and finding and selecting alternatives were the three key subprocesses of correct decision making.

The administrator is continually setting and resetting priorities and searching for new decision alternatives. The processes of decision making are limited, Simon asserted, by individuals' knowledge of the consequences of their choices and their preferences or motivations for one alternative over another. Simon recognized the practical limitations to human rationality, which he termed *bounded rationality.* The administrator "satisfices," that is, looks for a course of action that is satisfactory or "good enough." A choice is made without "maximizing," that is, first examining all possible behavior alternatives. Simon's contribution to organizational theory was his focus on the decision process and the human aspects of decision making. Traditional theories assumed complete rationality as the basis of decision making, but Simon drew attention to the bounded rationality of the process.

"Satisficing" is an interesting model to apply to decisions of correctional administrators. Often decisions in corrections are made based on a course of action that is "good enough." One example of satisficing might be an administrator who is worried about female correctional officers supervising male inmates. The administrator might decide to deploy the women in largely non-contact posts without considering that he or she may be denying the women opportunities to develop the confidence and skill to work with inmates. The administrator also may be reinforcing male coworkers' doubts about the women's abilities by making such a decision simply because it involves the least amount of effort but is adequate.

Etzioni's Structuralist Model. Etzioni (1975) attempted to integrate the classical management and behavioral theories in his structuralist model. He combined the structural (classical management theory) and the motivational (behavioral) perspectives in his analysis of power in an organization. Etzioni asserted that organizations require compliance from their members. The structural aspect of the organization is concerned with the type of power an organization uses to obtain conformity. The motivational aspect concerns the commitment of the employees to the goals of the organizational and thus their willingness to comply with organizational imperatives.

Etzioni described three types of leadership power: coercive, remunerative, and normative power. Coercive power depends on the potential application of physical force to make organizational members comply. Remunerative power comes from the manipulation of material resources, and rewards to increase the willingness of workers to comply. Normative power is based on the manipulation and allocation of symbols, such as love and prestige, to garner compliance. Etzioni's offering to organizational theory and management was to draw attention to the importance of the formal power structure and the human aspect of an organization in motivating employees.

Etzioni probably would have had a difficult time trying to describe leadership and the power base in a correctional institution, especially in light of conflicting, and often ambiguous, goals. Stojkovic et al. (1998) correctly observe that traditional types of power no longer promote effective administration in corrections. Coercive power and its potential threat have long been regarded as an ineffective method to obtain inmate compliance because of the sheer numbers of inmates in relation to officers. Changing conceptions of organizational dynamics between officers and inmates have pointed more to a sort of "negotiated order" with the consent of inmates. Knowing how to get along with people and how to interact in constructive ways are essential skills for correctional officers. The use of reward, rather than threats or coercion, as a base of power assumes a dominant role in shaping the behavior of inmates and gaining their compliance. In this way, a more positive culture may be shaped.

The Integrative Perspective

The integrative perspective integrated the structural and behavioral views of an organization and management with a consideration of external influences or the environment. Elements in these theories were blended to provide a more comprehensive explanation of an organization. The integrative approaches expanded organizational analysis to include a consideration of the larger economic, historical, political, and cultural framework. Leadership was viewed as contingent on organizational and environmental factors that determine a leader's control and influence. Effective leaders know how to manage their environment so that the leadership situation best fits their style. Systems theory and contingency theory are examples of the integrative perspective. The concept of reciprocity or exchange between the organization and its environment is central to the integrative theories.

Systems Theory. Traditional organizational theory tended to view the organization as a "closed system," isolated and unaffected by structure, processes, and organizations external to itself. This approach ignored the influence of the environment and organizational interaction with the environment. "Open-systems theory," on the other hand, focuses on the interrelationship of parts of a larger whole as they interact with each other and with their environment. Organizations obtain energy or information as input and export a product or service as output. An open system, therefore, involves a feedback system, the "flow of energy from the environment through the system itself and back into the environment" (Katz & Kahn, 1978). An organization has the capability for self-regulation and stability, or *homeostasis,* but it also must be able to change and adapt to new ideas, developments, and circumstances.

Open-systems theory emphasizes the interdependency and interrelatedness of the criminal justice system. What happens in one component, such as corrections, affects the other components such as law enforcement, prosecution, and the courts. While the inner workings of corrections is an important consideration, the permeability of the boundaries is a greater focus. Corrections does not exist in a vacuum, and what happens in the external environment affects its operations and the interactions between organizational members. The political, economic, and social environment cannot be ignored in any analysis of the functioning of the correctional organization.

To illustrate, the political climate of "get tough on sex offenders" and "protect society from sex offenders" has resulted in the passage of several sex offender specific laws, including registration, notification, and polygraph testing. These laws provide an excellent example of "system impact." They have an obvious effect on the work of the Department of Corrections (DOC). The DOC must notify law enforcement of an impending release of a sex offender who meets the provisions of the law, produce a special bulletin notification, and develop a supervisory plan. Law enforcement's task is face-to-face registration of the sex offender and deciding what level of notification is warranted. The community is also affected by the laws. They are alerted to the presence of a sex offender in their neighborhood through flyers, news media announcements, and/or a community notification meeting. Their level of anxiety may be heightened, and they may engage in self-protective behaviors or even vigilante acts against the offender.

Contingency Theory. Fiedler (1967) developed a theory of organizational leadership referred to as a contingency model. He maintained that effective leadership depended on the nature of the situation. He proposed that organizations should "engineer the job to fit the manager" and change the leadership situation to a more favorable one. He identified three features of any situation as determinant of the effectiveness of a leader: leader-member relations, task structure, and position power. Leader-member relations concern the extent to which workers respect leaders and are willing to follow their lead. Task structure refers to the degree to which the task is defined or structured. Position power is the official power of the leader to influence others in a desired direction. Fiedler asserts that depending on the combinations of these factors, certain leadership styles are more effective. For example, if there are poor leader-member relations, but the tasks are explicitly defined and the position power is strong, the leader needs to use a people-oriented approach.

Fiedler's theory is significant because he underscores the importance of flexibility and adaptation in leadership. Leadership style is contingent on the work situation and the relations among organizational members. Leaders must be attuned to the attitudes and values of organizational members and adjust their style accordingly. This flexibility and adaptability of leadership is congruent with a correctional work environment characterized by variability and complexity. A correctional leader must be aware of the prison culture and the orientation of workers toward organizational goals and the job itself. If line staff has developed values and work norms incongruent with the leader's goals, then the leader must have the ingenuity and resourcefulness to change their attitudes and to shape their work norms.

The Cognitive Perspective

The cognitive perspective views organizations as systems of shared meanings or systems of thought or cognitions. Here we see culture as a major organizing principle. An organization has a distinct culture with knowledge embodying the frames of reference that organizational members share. Culture is a product of the way individuals organize their experience to give it structure and meaning. Organizational culture has three levels: visible artifacts (visible organizational structures and processes); espoused values, rules, and behavioral norms; and tacit, basic underlying assumptions (unconscious, taken-for-granted beliefs, perceptions, thoughts, and feelings) (Schein, 1992). This view of an organization provides a means of understanding the culture of the organization and the rules or logic that guides action (Smircich, 1983).

A cognitive view of leadership posits that leaders influence the understandings and networks of meanings that others hold and express through behavior. In other words, leaders have a defining role in the culture of the workplace. Cultural leadership may involve creating cultures by attracting followers to the leader's cause and uniting them in purpose or mission. Trice and Beyer (1984) distinguish two types of leadership: cultural maintenance leadership and cultural innovation leadership. Cultural maintenance leadership is interested in maintaining the existing social structure and sustaining the mission and basic commitment of the group. Cultural innovation leadership involves a charismatic leader with a vision of innovation or change to the organizational structure. It may also involve culture maintenance with the leader reinforcing ideas already instilled in members and sustaining the mission and values. A leader uncovers the networks of meanings of organizational members in order to more effectively manage the organization.

In the cognitive perspective, an organization is perceived as a product of the mind, a system of shared thoughts or cognitions. The focus is on how members organize and use their culture to know how to function in the organization. An example of the cognitive perspective is symbolic organization theory.

Symbolic Organization Theory. In symbolic organization theory, the organization is seen as a system of shared symbols and meanings. This perspective focuses attention on the deeper structures of an organization and the covert layers of meaning shared by organizational participants (Jermier, Slocum, Fry, & Gaines, 1991). As these deeper structures are penetrated, the various forms of rituals, traditions, stories, and humor emerge. These forms may be consciously contrived to produce certain effects, such as an aggressive, competitive work environment, or may arise spontaneously to form patterns of meaning in areas of work (Morgan, Frost, & Pondy, 1983). Shared understandings and common modes of interpretation of experiences and events contribute to the stability or organization of group activity. "Organization is maintained through symbolic modes, such as language, that facilitate shared meaning and shared realities" (Smircich, 1983, p. 342).

The symbolic approach refers explicitly to an organizational culture. Shared beliefs and typical patterns dictate how an organization carries out its tasks and responsibilities. The *official organizational culture* refers to formally articulated mission statements and goals, standards of conduct, and rules and regulations. An *organizational subculture* consists of shared understandings about the organization's mission and standards of behavior, as well as shared understandings of practices and norms that develop in a group of employees. Organizational subcultures emerge as groups of employees challenge, modify, or even replace the formal culture (Jermier et al., 1991, p. 172).

In corrections, the formal prison culture is militaristic with symbols of superordination and subordination (e.g., insignia, shirt color, and titles). While management may view these symbols as representative of order and authority, workers may see the symbols as representative of their own inferiority and inability to make decisions without conferring with supervisors. Another example is the movement to professionalize corrections that includes endorsement of baccalaureate degrees and postgraduate education among correctional officers. This may serve to discourage line officers who found the school experience difficult and even stressful or who simply do not have the time or inclination to complete school. For the officers, this may create two cultures, with one composed of officers who meet the educational expectations and others who feel they cannot.

The Transformational Perspective

The transformational perspective deals with organizational change. It is a new way of viewing an organization, not as an independent entity, but as the product of a prevailing agreement in consciousness or a paradigm (Banner & Gagne,

1995). According to Levy and Merry (1986), transformational theories share three common characteristics. First, the major purpose is to change the underlying assumptions, worldview, or paradigm of the organization and to introduce a new paradigm. Second, this is accomplished through the creation of a vision, ideas, or direction that transcends the confines of the current paradigm. Finally, these theories focus on the organizational members' perceptions of reality and what shapes them.

Many of the transformational theories recognize the importance of leadership as being instrumental for organizational change. Transformational theory views cultural leadership as a dynamic, active process. A transformational leader sees the organization as part of a larger, organic whole and creates a shared vision of the whole organization as an organizing principle for the parts (Bass, 1985). Tichy and Devanna (1986) define transformational leaders as change agents and risk takers who believe in people and try to empower others. Transformational leadership characteristics include charisma, individualized consideration, and intellectual stimulation of workers (Bass, Waldman, Avolio, & Bebb, 1987). Organizational members trust the vision of the leader and develop emotional feelings toward the leader.

In this theoretical perspective, organizational change is natural. It is a continuous process in response to changing external and internal conditions (Leifer, 1989). This theory suggests that the presence of instabilities in an organization does not necessarily lead to chaos, but instead offers the opportunity for transformation in both style and behavior. The success of an organization will depend on rekindling faith and optimism in the organization's potential for survival. Transformation theory focuses on how the organization can meet the needs of employees so that they feel a sense of belonging and investment in the organization and can realize their full potential.

The transformational correctional leader engenders a culture with a shared vision for the members of the organization. That vision is conveyed and reinforced on a continuous basis through formal means (e.g., directives, literature, rituals) and informal ways (e.g., group discussions and team approaches). The leader monitors the sentiments of the officers to ensure congruency with the vision. The leader is actively involved in creating, shaping, and even transforming the officers' views to that vision. As an example, a correctional leader may have a vision of a collaborative, idea-sharing team committed to working with the increasing numbers of mentally ill in correctional institutions. The officers may have the attitude that the mentally ill are the "dregs of society" and that their job is not to "babysit" or coddle mentally ill inmates. The leader may work to change these attitudes through strategies such as discussions on mental illness and the challenges of working with this population. The leader shows a continuing interest in the officers' work and often sits in on team meetings. This sends the message that their work is valued and that the goal is to provide quality ser-vices to the mentally ill.

ORGANIZATIONAL AND MANAGEMENT THEORIES: CONCLUDING COMMENTS

Several theoretical perspectives on organizations and management have been presented in this chapter. The intent was to consider the contributions, as well as the limitations, of these perspectives on organizations, management, and leadership. Theories in the structural perspective concentrated on the activities of workers and management, their functions for the organization, and their connection to the whole, but neglected any conceptualization of a work culture within an organization. The behavioral perspective accentuated the human aspects of an organization as the key to maintaining an organization and contributed to the development of a cultural theory based on the relationships among organizational members. The intregrative view considered the influence of environmental factors, including historical, political, economic, and sociological variables, in its analysis of an organization.

Organizational theory also has emphasized the internal components and processes of an organization: the formal structure, work culture, and the interaction of organizational members that shape its culture. The cognitive perspective viewed the culture of an organization as manifested in shared meanings, symbols, values, and ideologies. The significance of culture for organizational analysis was revealed in an examination of the assumptions of these theories. The transformational view centered on changing or shaping the formal structure and the underlying assumptions and values of organization's culture to fit a new, transformational worldview.

From these theories we explored the development of thought from a focus on the structural features to a realization of the human aspects of an organization. The inquiry moved beyond the formal elements of an organization to its workplace culture(s). We learned how the role of management evolved from a supervisor concerned with the efficiency and control of workers to a manager concerned with employee job satisfaction and motivation. We also saw how management and leadership are actually two very different conceptualizations. The manager guides, directs, and coordinates the work activities of his or her employees. The leader plays a more dynamic, inspirational role in shaping and transforming the culture of an organization. Finally, we observed how the view of an organization as a closed system changed to that of an entity actively interacting with its environment.

AN INTEGRATED APPROACH TO ORGANIZATIONAL CULTURE

In conceptualizing an organization and its culture, we propose an integrated perspective that is more comprehensive and inclusive than previous theories. The integration of theoretical perspectives has been described as "the combination of two or more pre-existing theories based on their perceived commonalities, into a single reformulated theoretical model with greater comprehensiveness and explanatory value than any one of its component theories" (Farnworth, 1989, p. 95). We propose a theoretical model that extracts certain concepts from organizational, management, and leadership theory to provide a more comprehensive and complete understanding of an organization and its culture.

Our model brings culture and cultural leadership to the fore. Drawing from symbolic organization theory, our theory of leadership emphasizes three aspects of an organization: formal culture, informal culture, and individual organizational members. The formal or "official" culture includes the formal structure and official goals, mission statement, conduct expectations, and leadership style. Weber's model helps us to comprehend the influence of this bureaucratic structure on the formation of a culture. The informal culture, on the other hand, consists of shared understandings of procedures and norms that develop among groups of workers as they interpret the formal goals and standards within the practicalities and realities of their work experience. The attitudes, beliefs, and values from the unique histories and experiences of individual workers are another component. These attitudes and experiences are then shaped by the workers' experience in the organization while working and relating to other members. Thus, the principles of behavioral theories also have influenced our model.

Human interaction creates and perpetuates a culture, so a leader must understand the relationships among organizational members. The divergence between formally articulated goals and values and the attitudes developed and molded by work reality is crucial for leadership. Leadership also must have the ability and the vision to create, shape, and transform a culture. Finally, as systems theory demonstrated, the impact of external influences (e.g., the courts, politics, and economics) on corrections is important to remember. Therefore, the relationship of external influences to the formal structure and culture of the organization is a key consideration in our analysis. We include an analysis of the historical and environmental context of the organization and its role in shaping the organization's character and culture. The history of the organization encompasses the development of the organization in relation to such factors as philosophy, structure, and style of leadership. Environmental influences include the economic, social, legal, and political aspects that have an impact on the functioning and maintenance of the organization.

Cultural leadership is the focal point in our theoretical orientation. The role of leaders in developing, maintaining, and transforming a culture is central to our theory. Leaders attempt to coalesce differing perspectives, assumptions, and values of members into a more congruent work group. In this way, the organizational performance of the members is directed by leadership. Leaders inspire and stimulate members to be aware of the vision and mission of the organization. According to transformation theory, this may involve a change or transformation of existing sentiments among workers. This change is facilitated by inspirational and motivational influences. Specific strategies will be discussed at length in Chapters 6 and 7.

While leaders shape the culture of the organization, there also are multiple influences on leadership. We will examine those influences, as well as strategies for leaders to use in circumventing or more effectively managing their impact. Leaders can choose to direct and shape the culture, or to be directed and defined by it. In our theory, leaders assume a dynamic and vital role in developing and influencing the orientation, values, and work performance of organizational members.

This cultural framework for organizations and management moves us in the direction of questioning taken-for-granted assumptions, raises issues of context and meaning, and brings to the surface underlying values in an organization (Smircich, 1983). In focusing on culture, we focus on higher-order processes, language, and the creation of meaning. In a cultural analysis, an organization is viewed as a particular form of human expression rather than as a purposeful instrument or adaptive mechanism (Smircich, 1983). An organization becomes a dynamic culture of values, norms, and beliefs that give shape, direction, and uniqueness to it. A cultural approach to leadership yields new insights into organizations by uncovering networks of meanings contained in ideologies, norms, and values (Trice & Beyer, 1984).

Schein (1992) distinguishes leadership from management because of the leader's unique function in creating, managing, and changing culture. Leadership is more than simply coordinating and influencing the work activities of the organization. It is developing, maintaining, or changing the culture of the organization. In the next chapter we apply our integrative perspective to the correctional organization in order to more completely understand the complexity and uniqueness of the correctional organization's culture and the role of leadership in maintaining or molding that culture.

CASE SCENARIO *Leadership—Motivation and Culture*

When Joe Denton began working at Rappaport Correctional Institution, he was hired as a unit manager of a 250-bed segregation unit. He was intrigued about working in institutional corrections after spending 10 years as a supervisor of a mental health unit in probation and parole. Denton had several ideas for improvement and was eager to implement them. Concerned about the number of mentally disordered inmates on the "seg" unit, he decided their management would be his major focus. Warden Butz assured Joe that he would have his full support as well as the freedom to carry out his plans.

The third week after Denton was hired, he called a meeting with the correctional staff. He anticipated that the officers would be wary of him, since he was new to the unit and to the prison. He also expected some resistance to his ideas, especially since they would mean more work for the staff. Denton decided he would come on "strong" with a no-nonsense approach. At the meeting, he informed the officers that he had a new way of doing things and he expected their full cooperation. Denton stated that he expected a more professional attitude from them. He proceeded to outline his ideas, and then spelled out his expectations in detail.

First, Denton wanted his staff to have more interaction with the inmates, so that the officers could more adequately assess the mental state of

(continued)

Case Scenario continued

the seg inmates and whether the inmates were taking their medication. He then directed the officers to keep more detailed daily logs of inmate-staff interaction and the daily activities of inmates. Denton noted their faulty record keeping and the disorganization of their paperwork. He emphasized the importance of this record keeping in managing the large number of mentally ill inmates on the seg unit. He ended the meeting with the directive that all correctional staff were considered a part of the treatment team and should act accordingly.

As the weeks passed, Denton noticed that the correctional staff was very reserved in their manner toward him. He was businesslike in return, and was secretly relieved that he didn't have to listen to their complaints. The daily logs were checked on a periodic basis, and although Denton noticed some improvement, he was irritated that there wasn't a more significant showing. He decided that he needed to be more directive in his approach, and he called another meeting.

At the next meeting, Denton reproached the officers for their uncooperative attitude and lack of professionalism. He used examples from the daily logs to highlight mistakes and poor recording of information. Then, glancing around the table and seeing the expressionless faces of his staff, he lost his temper and called his officers lazy and incompetent.

Case Scenario Questions

1. Think about the management or leadership theories presented in this chapter. What type of manager is Joe Denton? What are his assumptions about his correctional staff, and how do these assumptions influence his interactions with the officers?

2. Again, think about the motivational theories reviewed in this chapter. The correctional staff on the segregation unit at Rappaport Correctional Institution appeared unwilling or unmotivated to implement the changes proposed by Denton. Why? What could Denton have done differently to gain their cooperation?

3. What type of work culture is the segregation unit? What could Denton do to change this culture?

REFERENCES

Banner, D. K., & Gagne, T. E. (1995). *Designing effective organizations.* Thousand Oaks, CA: Sage.

Barnard, C. (1938). *The functions of an executive.* Cambridge, MA: Harvard University Press.

Bass, B. M. (1985). *Leadership and performance beyond expectations.* New York: Free Press.

Bass, B. M. & Avolio, B. J. (1994). *Improving organizational effectiveness through transformational leadership.* Thousand Oaks, CA: Sage.

Bass, B. M., Waldman, D. A., Avolio, B. J., & Bebb, M. (1987). Transformational leadership and the falling dominoes effect. *Group and Organization Studies, 12*(1), 73–87.

Etzioni, A. (1975). *A comparative analysis of complex organizations.* New York: Free Press.

Farkas, M. (1998). The normative code among correctional officers: An exploration of components and functions. *Journal of Crime and Justice, 22*(1), 23–36.

Farnworth, M. (1989). Theory integration vs. model building. In S. F. Messner, M. D. Krohn, & A. E. Liska (Eds.), *Theoretical integration in the study of deviance and crime* (pp. 93–100). Albany, NY: State University of New York Press.

Fayol, H. (1949). *General and industrial management*. London: Sir Isaac Pitman & Sons.

Fiedler, F. E. (1967). *A theory of leadership effectiveness*. New York: McGraw-Hill.

Herzberg, F. (1966). *Work and the nature of man*. Cleveland, OH: World Publishing.

Herzberg, F., Mausner, B., & Synderman, B. B. (1959). *The motivation to work*. New York: Wiley.

Jermier, J., Slocum, J. W., Fry, L., & Gaines, J. (1991). Organizational subcultures in a soft bureaucracy: Resistance behind the myth and facade of an official culture. *Organization Science, 2*(2), 170–194.

Johnson, R. (1996). *Hard time*. Belmont, CA: Wadsworth.

Katz, D., & Kahn, R. L. (1978). *The social psychology of organizations* (2d. ed.). New York: Wiley.

Leifer, R. (1989). Understanding organizational transformation using a dissipative structure model. *Human Relations, 42,* 899–916.

Levy, A., & Merry, U. (1986). *Organizational transformation*. New York: Praeger.

Maslow, A. (1954). *Motivation and personality*. New York: Harper & Row.

Mayo, E. (1933). *The human problems of an industrial civilization*. Cambridge, MA: Murray Printing.

McGregor, D. (1967). *The professional manager*. New York: McGraw-Hall.

Morgan, G., Frost, P. J., & Pondy, L. R. (1983). Organizational symbolism. In L. R. Pondy, P. J. Frost, G. Morgan, & T. Dandridge (Eds.), *Organizational symbolism* (pp. 3–33). Greenwich, CT: JAI Press.

Schein, E. H. (1992). *Organizational culture and leadership*. San Francisco: Jossey-Bass.

Schein, E. H. (1993). What is culture? In P. J. Frost, L. F. Moore, C. C. Lundberg, & J. Martin (Eds.), *Reframing organizational culture* (pp. 243–253). Newbury Park, CA: Sage.

Simon, H. A. (1947). *Administrative behavior: A study of decision-making process in administrative organizations*. New York: Macmillan.

Smircich, L. (1983) Concepts of culture and organization analysis. *Administrative Science Quarterly, 28,* 339–358.

Stojkovic, S., Kalinich, D., & Klofas, J. (1998). *Criminal justice organizations: Administration and management* (2nd ed.). Belmont, CA: West/Wadsworth.

Taylor, F. W. (1911). *Principles of scientific management*. New York: Harper & Brothers.

Tichy, N. M., & Devanna, M. A. (1986). *The transformational leader*. New York: Wiley.

Trice, H. M., & Beyer, J. M. (1984). Studying organizational culture through rites, rituals and ceremonies. *Academy of Management Review, 9*(4), 653–667.

Weber, M. *The theory of social and economic organization*. New York: Oxford University Press.

CORRECTIONAL CULTURE

The preceding chapter explored the development of organization theory and management and leadership theory. The concept of an organizational culture was introduced as an integral component to our theory. We defined culture as an amalgam of relationships with other organizational members. It is manifested in the meanings and sentiments shared by interacting social actors. Correctional officers, for example, develop understandings of organizational values and accepted modes of action based on their relationships with colleagues, supervisors, and inmates. These sentiments are also molded by an organization's history, leadership, and a variety of factors, such as age and size of an organization, and the interplay between the structural and cultural elements. Subcultures emerge as officers develop, perpetuate, and affirm norms and values in their relationships with colleagues. Colleagues serve as a point of reference in order for officers to orient themselves to their roles within the prison organization. Relationships with inmates and supervisors also influence the formation and perpetuation of an officer culture.

The challenge for an understanding of the correctional culture is to capture the shared sentiments, values, and norms of officers, while still recognizing individual variation. The realization that culture may exist at multiple levels and that there may be multiple cultures at the same level is an important conceptualization. Finally, the role and influence of leadership in creating, sustaining, and transforming culture must be discerned.

We begin our analysis of the culture of correctional work by examining the development of thought on this culture. Three basic conceptual schemes emerge from the literature. Early research relied on a unitary model: a predominant subculture of officers with negative views toward inmates and a procustodial orientation. The second model recognized the differentiation among officers and proposed various typologies of officers based on certain variables, such as shift, career stage, and orientation toward inmates. The third model proposed three cultures in the prison organization: the culture of officers as distinct from that of middle management and top corrections officials. We will look closely at these three conceptualizations and extract the elements that are useful for our understanding of the culture of correctional work.

THE UNITARY CULTURAL MODEL

Much of the early literature on correctional officers contains references to a unitary "subculture" of guards with a unique set of values and norms. This subcultural understanding was influenced by the formal definition of the guard role at that time in history. Prior to 1956, the guard role was more clearly defined—maintaining security and internal order and controlling inmates. However, the degree to which the guards carried out these functions was the basis of the subculture. Informal values of toughness, anti-inmate sentiments, and adherence to informal rules of how to "handle" inmates and how to "run their cell blocks and units" characterized the subculture. Guards felt isolated from supervisory personnel and alone in their everyday management of inmates. And supervisory staff viewed their role as simply overseeing guards. They allowed guards wide latitude in handling inmates as long as the formal rules were followed. In most cases, they were not attuned to the realities of correctional work, which maintained the chasm between guards and supervisors. The unionization of guards also may have unwittingly contributed to an "us versus them" attitude and the formation of subcultures within the correctional organization.

This unitary view remained popular until researchers such as Klofas and Toch (1982) began to question its viability and utility as a model for understanding the work behavior of correctional officers. In their study of four maximum security prisons, they found that "subcultural custodians"—officers with a shared anti-inmate, procustodial orientation—were actually in the minority of officers. Interestingly enough, though "subcultural custodians" were few, they believed they were in the majority of officers. They assumed their anti-inmate perspective was consensually shared. Other officers also believed that these subcultural custodians were in the majority. In other words, the subcultural custodians were a small subgroup of officers, and not a dominant prevailing group characterizing the officer culture.

Klofas (1984) reexamined this notion of a singular, custodial subculture among correctional officers. He argued convincingly against such a subculture for several reasons: (1) this concept of subculture neglects or "masks" the variability between officers and other groups in the prison organization; (2) where common beliefs are identified, they are often opposite those predicted in the subculture model; (3) officers are neither homogeneous nor different enough from other workers to be viewed as a subculture; and (4) applying the concept of a subculture offers only an uncomplimentary stereotype for analyzing personnel issues. Klofas contended that applying the concept of an anti-inmate, procustodial subculture does not recognize the diversity among officers and their potential contributions to correctional work other than simple custodial tasks.

The power of this unitary subcultural view is that it adversely affects the relationships between all organizational members. Acting on prison lore, inmates view officers as "hacks" and "screws" and interact with them accordingly. They balk at orders, challenge correctional authority, and encourage other inmates to respond similarly. Correctional officers perceive their role to be that of "keeper" and relate to inmates in a custodial fashion. To behave in any other way toward inmates would not be appropriate and would bring the condemnation of their colleagues. Furthermore, their job performance is inhibited and their aspirations are limited to primarily custodial tasks. As Klofas (1984) argues, management will see officers as an "undifferentiated mass whose contributions are limited to security" (p. 172). Their interest in human service will remain untapped and a hidden agenda for officers. Moreover, this unitary view also negates the potential of correctional leaders to create, shape, and transform not only these attitudes, but also the character of relationships and, ultimately, the culture of correctional work.

TYPOLOGIES OF OFFICERS

The second perspective on the culture of correctional work emphasized individual variation among officers. Researchers looked at several variables, including orientation toward inmates and colleagues and career stage, in order to actually classify officers. For the sake of convenience, we have simplified the extensive amount of research on types by identifying a number of similar types in the literature. Much of the literature on types of corrections officers demonstrates the polarity between a custodial identity and function and a rehabilitative or human service identity and function that was promulgated by the introduction of rehabilitative philosophy to the field of corrections.

If one envisions a continuum of officers, the "custodian" would be at one end and the "human service officer" at the other. In the typology theories, we revisit the custodian from the unitary subcultural model, which further illustrates the power of this negative stereotype. The "custodian/subcultural custodian" (Klofas & Toch, 1982), "hard ass" (Kauffman, 1988), or "John Wayne–Clint Eastwood type" (Owen, 1988) perceives correctional work as primarily custodial and emphasizes the themes of coercive authority, toughness, and social distance. The officer's "tough facade" is also present in relations with fellow officers. Fear of rejection and a desire to be "one of the boys" promotes the adoption of a custodial role. According to Owen (1988), this type is out to gain as much status and power within the hierarchy as possible through tough, authoritarian relations with inmates. This officer type tends to be a newer officer and to work on the night shift.

The "human service officer" or "people worker" (Johnson, 1996), "supported majority" (Klofas & Toch, 1982), "white hat" (Kauffman, 1988), or "professional correctional officer" (Owen, 1988) is another predominant social type and the polar opposite of the aforementioned custodial type. Johnson (1996) contends that officers have a private agenda or latent identity in which they seek to enrich their jobs through decreased social distance from inmates and personalized relations. They desire to provide human services and refer inmates to appropriate services and programs; however, they perceive other officers as custodial, which inhibits their feelings of human service (Lombardo, 1989). "Many of these officers get lonely as closet social workers and assume a custodial pose to secure companionship and support" (Johnson & Price, 1981). These officers hold positive attitudes toward inmates and rely on interpersonal skills rather than coercion in their interactions with inmates. They seek to advise, support, console, refer, and generally try to assist inmates with institutional and personal problems (Johnson & Price, 1981).

Another major type is the "functionary" (Kauffman, 1988), "ritualist" (Crouch & Marquart, 1983) or "just doing the job" type (Owen, 1988). Kauffman (1988) indicates that officers transition from one type to another as a reflection of a socialization process and their own moral transformations. As officers become socialized into the prison environment, they search for justifications for their emerging hostility and negativism toward inmates. "Functionaries" anesthetize themselves from feeling sympathy or kindness toward inmates. They have no inclination to strictly enforce rules or to incorporate more human service activities. They are ambivalent or, worse, indifferent to inmates and officers. They insulate themselves from the social reality of prison by simply going through the motions or "functions" of the job and not getting involved.

The "burnout" (Kauffman, 1988) or "discouraged subculturalist" (Klofas & Toch, 1982) is another type in the literature. The "burnout" holds a negative orientation toward inmates, officers, and the administration; these officers have a basic mistrust and hostility toward all three groups. Paranoia characterizes relations with inmates, while relations with fellow officers are strained. Such officers are unable to cope with the realities of working in prison. The experience of being a correctional officer dominates their behavior; they tend to behave and experience the same feelings outside the prison. "Burnouts" remain in the job for the extrinsic rewards of compensation and benefits.

Zimmer (1986) examined approaches to the job among female officers. The author claimed that with the increasing numbers of women entering correctional work, distinct roles have emerged among female prison guards in response to problems basic to the job and to women in a nontraditional, predominantly male job. She described three patterns of adaptation or roles identified by women working in men's prisons: the institutional, modified, and inventive roles.

The "institutional role" refers to those officers who adhere closely to the formal rules established by the administration and stressed during academy training. They strive to perform their jobs on an equal basis with male officers, and hence minimize their female status and maximize social distance in their interactions with inmates, coworkers, and supervisors.

Female officers in the second type, the "modified role," feel hostility toward female guards who demand equal treatment. These women prefer to work on posts involving less direct contact with inmates because of a belief in their physical limitations and the impropriety of having female guards see nude male inmates. They rely on the assistance and protection of male officers in performing their duties, and they prefer assignments to less threatening posts by supervisors.

The "inventive role" represents the third type of female correctional officer identified by Zimmer (1986). These women prefer less social distance from inmates, and seek opportunities for increased interaction. They have integrated counseling into their job, either to better perform their control functions or to help inmates. Because of their good relationships with inmates and perceived lenient rule enforcement, women in the inventive role have antagonistic relationships with male colleagues.

Although these typologies contribute to an appreciation of individual variation in approach and style among correctional officers, they have significant shortcomings. Typologies may be too rigid as conceptualization schemes. Spontaneity is overlooked, and the ability of officers to change their outlook, reconsider certain values and common practices, and develop or foster improved relations with other organizational members is left unexplored. While the unitary model overemphasizes cohesiveness in the culture with little flexibility or room for individual variation, typologies present a rather fragmented culture with little hope of developing cohesion and a shared mission or purpose among officers.

THE THREE-CULTURES MODEL

In understanding the culture of correctional work, it is important to realize that the culture among officers may be distinct from that of management and top correctional officials, and that there may be multiple subcultures among officers. Some researchers have applied a "three-cultures" perspective to illuminate the organizational culture of corrections. Farkas and Manning (1997) proposed a framework for analyzing the culture to illustrate the values, sentiments, and modes of thinking of each segment of the organization. In this conceptualization, the correctional organization is divided into segments: the "lower participant" or officer segment, the middle management segment, and the top command segment. This perspective is useful in describing the position of line officers in relation to the "higher" decision-making segments in the hierarchy and the unique concerns of each segment that affect their relations with one another.

The line officer segment of a correctional organization is occupied by those holding the rank of sergeant or below. The majority of these officers belong to a union. They are oriented internally to what occurs inside the organization. Supervision of inmates and maintaining order in cellblocks or pod units, on work details, and in recreational areas, industrial shops, and school are the primary tasks of officers.

Individuals become officers after a relatively brief period, an average of five to nine weeks, in training. In terms of job skills, the emphasis is on concrete knowledge—hands-on experience and on-the-job training. This fosters the idea that management and the general public cannot possibly understand the task complexities and realities of correctional work because they are not working "on-the-line" with inmates. Officers generally have little input into decision making and feel that management cannot understand the reality of their work situation (Cheek & Miller, 1982, 1983).

The officer segment feels alienated from management, and even more isolated from top command. Their status at the bottom of the prison hierarchy is conveyed through cultural artifacts, such as the color of their uniform shirts and the number of insignia. Indeed, middle management is often referred to as "white shirts" by line staff. It is not unusual to walk through a prison and overhear a line officer warn a coworker that a white shirt is coming.

Line officers also feel isolated and alienated from coworkers (Cheek & Miller, 1982). "Conflicts over definitions of the job and working styles may divide the workers among themselves" (Owen, 1988, p. 22). Some officers believe a tough, custodial posture is the way to handle inmates, while others prefer a more communicative, interpersonal style. Poole and Regoli (1981) identified two features of the correctional officer role that inhibit the development of extensive work camaraderie and in-group solidarity: (1) interaction with coworkers is minimal, limited to brief periods of contact in the dining room, at shift end, or staffings; and (2) officers are expected to perform the functions of their particular work assignments alone.

The middle-management segment is typically stagnated at the rank and perhaps still hoping to rise. Depending on their management style, they may identify with either line officers or top command. Middle management often serves as a link between line officers and administrators, interpreting policies and directives. They are internally oriented; their concern is with maintaining order and security in the prison, and hence ensuring that line officers are doing their jobs. "When they are not responding to trouble, the lieutenants roam about the institution making checks and shakedowns on inmates and lower-ranking guards" (Jacobs & Retsky, 1980, p. 183). Middle management is responsible for disciplinary write-ups and for evaluating the job performance of line officers. They also may investigate inmate allegations against officers. Activities are conducted with an "eye" for promotion.

The warden and the administration occupy the top command in the hierarchy. "The top command segment rarely have time to exercise first-hand supervision of the general prison area" (Jacobs & Retsky, 1980, p. 199). For those in the upper levels of the hierarchy, concerns with inmates are secondary (Owen, 1988). Concerns with line officers also may be of secondary importance with the exception of union issues. Instead, those at the top are consumed by administrative duties and paperwork. The top command in a correctional organization, like that in the police organization, is oriented to "external audiences" and making the right political connections (Stojkovic, Kalinich, & Klofas, 1998).

Prison administrators are "answerable" to a variety of external and internal groups. Prison reform groups, legislative bodies, the media, and the courts are some of the major external groups that constrain the policies and decisions of administrators. For instance, many policies and procedures are either court-mandated or developed within court-mandated guidelines.

Moreover, the top command segment must "answer" to internal audiences. The department/division of corrections and employee unions are the primary internal groups affecting the actions of administrators. Irwin and Austin (1997) claim that with the more centralized approach to managing contemporary prisons, administrators no longer have the autonomy and discretion they once possessed. They now defer to the regulations and procedures imposed by the central office (the department/division of corrections). Administrators also must consider the interests of unions in their management processes. Relationships between employees and the administration are now more formalized, with the rights and obligations of each side stipulated by a labor contract (Clear & Cole, 1994).

The three-cultures model has value in the way it highlights the major issues of each segment of the prison organization. The commonality of these concerns is lost in the analysis, however. The idea that leadership of the top command might share similar concerns with line officers is not considered. The three-cultures model neglects the role of leadership in transcending the cultural barriers of three segments and in developing a shared mission, shared values, and shared understandings of the complexities of each segment's tasks.

WHERE DO WE GO FROM HERE?— THREE CULTURES AND BEYOND

Research has taken the analysis of correctional culture down a rather narrow path. We are left with three distinct approaches to viewing correctional culture, and as we have suggested, these views by themselves do not allow us to appreciate the richness with which culture can be understood and, more importantly, influenced by correctional leaders. The three discrete representations of culture, however, serve as a point of departure upon which a more thorough analysis of correctional culture can be achieved. We extend the analysis provided by these earlier approaches to take into consideration significant views we introduced in Chapter 2. These views actually reveal the importance of the contributions of a number of schools of thought on organizational culture and their relevance to correctional organizations.

Our integrative model of understanding correctional culture is rooted in the early theoretical views of culture as presented by the bureaucratic model, the behavioral models, the human relations and interactions perspective, the systems model, and a broader ecological view that considers the importance of environment to correctional systems. Our review of this literature has moved us in the direction of accepting that correctional culture is highly influenced by the necessity of the bureaucratic approach to organizing large numbers of people, the effect of formal systems on correctional employees, and more importantly, how informal modes of adaptation are created in reaction to formal control mechanisms among correctional staff, and how the external world and the environment impact corrections in very direct and indirect ways.

An integrated model of correctional culture, therefore, can be understood on two dimensions. First, by recognizing that there are many cultures within correctional organizations, we can direct efforts toward unifying these cultures to achieve consistency in practice and operations. Correctional officers, for example, exhibit specific norms, attitudes, and beliefs, as research has documented, yet these representations of a specific culture cannot be in opposition to the larger goals of the organization if the organization is to function effectively. Clearly, officers, as a group, may disagree with middle managers and administrative staff about the best possible practices to accomplish tasks, achieve objectives, and pursue goals, but everyone must be clear about what the organization is attempting to achieve. The research on goal ambiguity and role conflict within prison organizations has demonstrated clearly that arriving at a consensus on these matters is a difficult and daunting task; nevertheless, for the organization to function, some consensus and unity of mission is essential.

This is why correctional leadership is so critical and essential to prison organizations. Whether the mission is defined around the parameters of security and control (DiIulio, 1987) or based on a human service mandate (Johnson, 1996), the central purpose of leadership is to provide inspiration and direction so that the mission is transmitted to correctional employees and accepted by the various cultures of the organization. This no small feat, given how other types of concerns, constraints, and factors shape and influence what correctional leaders can and cannot do.

For example, in the past 10 years, due to political demands from their environment, correctional leaders have bitten off more than they can chew. They have in some instances made promises or acquiesced to specific demands from their political environment that has actually made correctional leadership more difficult. A glaring example of this is the rather passive approach that many correctional leaders have taken when faced with burgeoning prisoner populations over the past decade. For many correctional administrators, there has been no attempt to speak truth to political power by relaying the problems that increased prisoner populations create for their institutions. Many correctional administrators have accepted their lot by developing more elaborate and detailed budgeting and *management* initiatives to stave off the prisoner onslaught, but very few have actually acted like *leaders* and questioned the efficacy of incarcerating unmanageable numbers of offenders in their prisons. Very few have wanted to question the status quo and actually *lead* by raising the question of whether an imprisonment binge (Irwin & Austin, 1997) is an appropriate strategy to pursue in dealing with crime. Through their abdication, correctional administrators have actually made their lives and the lives of correctional staff worse and further polarized correctional cultures in opposition to themselves. In short, they have made correctional leadership even more difficult and, in some cases, completely impossible.

Through a recognition of the varied cultures within correctional organizations, leaders can begin to define their mission and where they want to be in the future. Some writers on organizations, like Nanus (1992), refer to this as visionary leadership. For correctional leaders, the question becomes what do they want their correctional organizations to achieve, and how do the various cultures of the organization either accept or reject their vision. In Chapter 5, we will discuss how correctional leaders can develop a mission statement and vision for their organizations. For now, we want to stress that *a unification of competing cultures through a mission statement that employees can agree on is the central task for correctional leaders*. This activity cannot begin until there is a recognition that a unitary cultural view of correctional organizations is too narrow and ultimately lacks an appreciation of others and their interests. Through a mission statement, however, correctional leaders can overcome resistance among employees and unify their organizations so that they can move forward toward agreed-upon paths and mutually acceptable goals.

The second dimension of understanding correctional culture recognizes that the environment is critical to a leader's success or failure. Past discussions of correctional leadership have focused too much on the management end of correctional work. Earlier works have stressed management approaches and ways of structuring the prison environment so that staff can be more effective (DiIulio, 1987; Houston, 1999). These matters are important, yet the discussions have either downplayed or minimized the importance of environment to both correctional leadership and correctional management. Our integrated model of correctional culture suggests that understanding and working with the environment is of critical importance to effective correctional leadership. What is astounding is that many correctional leaders understand this fundamental point, but few do anything to improve their skills so they will be more competitive and effective in dealing with significant actors in their environment (Breed, 1998).

By environment, we mean not only politicians and political bodies, such as state legislatures, but also the courts, private foundations, public interest groups, and political parties, to mention a few. In theory, the environment could mean anyone outside the boundaries of the correctional organization, although not everyone is a critical or pivotal actor within the environment. Some environmental influences are more important than others (we will examine the role of environmental influences on correctional leadership in Chapter 5). Nevertheless, the significance of the environment has been lost in many discussions of correctional leadership, even though it plays such an important part in what correctional leaders can and cannot do with their organizations.

DiIulio (1991) was correct when he stated that correctional leaders need to be in their positions long enough to have an impact on their agencies, but *how* they perform in their role as a correctional leader is even more important—especially how they manipulate their environment in such a way as to make their mission statement and vision real possibilities. Correctional leaders cannot completely control their environments, but they can have more of an impact than they currently have. Too often correctional leaders have denied their own responsibility in shaping their environment and claimed that their hands are tied, that governors are unyielding, that legislatures are uncontrollable—in short, that they can only react to their problems, not influence their environments. Such a defeatist position has not served correctional leaders well. In fact, taking a limited and reactive position vis-à-vis the environment has actually exacerbated correctional leadership; it has made correctional work more difficult for staff, and it has compounded correctional problems.

We need to rethink correctional leadership and replace the reactive posture with a proactive approach. Such an approach recognizes the environment as critical to the success of correctional organizations and enhances an understanding among correctional staff of how stakeholders in the environment do not have to be enemies or pariahs. It seeks out partnerships with the environment to make the mission of correctional organizations known as well as integrated into a common understanding of how corrections fits into a larger picture of crime management and reduction. In short, *effective correctional leaders have a vision of where they want to be in relation to their environment.*

Through visionary leadership, correctional leaders can address the two dimensions discussed earlier: competing cultures and environment. Correctional leaders who have some idea of where they want their organization to be in the future are able to inspire employees across competing correctional cultures to come together around a set of values and ideas they feel are relevant to them. In addition, correctional leaders with a vision are able to transmit to the environment where they want to be and, more importantly, what they value as an organization. Through visionary practices, correctional leaders can enlist support for their programs. They will also engender detractors and critics of their ideas, but this is not a bad thing. It is a risk of effective leadership. Correctional leaders must state what they, their organization, and their employees stand for and where they want to be. Without such a statement, they are rudderless and oftentimes left to the vagaries of the political winds.

The dissatisfaction of many correctional professionals can be traced to the lack of a sense of purpose and vision in their leaders. Without such guidance, many correctional staff do not see any ultimate meaning in their work. Without vision at the top of the organization, correctional employees are left to their own devices in figuring out what the prison is trying to achieve. In some cases, this leads to unacceptable behaviors and further erosion of organizational culture into an "us-against-them" posture, again with competing cultures vying for control of the organization. As one correctional administrator commented to one of the authors of this text: "We have no leaders in the department of corrections, only mediocre managers. Many of our so-called leaders are stuck in doing whatever the governor wants or whatever politician has a pet project he wants put into place. In many cases, these ideas are nonsense and everyone knows it, including central administration, but they don't have the guts to question anything because they don't know what they stand for."

The primary question for correctional leaders is, what do we stand for? Moreover, they must ask, how do our values represent or deviate from the values of our employees and their respective cultures, and those of our stakeholders? Without visionary leadership, correctional leaders are left in the reactive mode, which precludes them from actually leading. Answering such fundamental questions is critical to leading correctional organizations, yet few correctional leaders are asking or addressing them. Correctional leaders have failed to see how important visionary leadership is to working with the competing cultures in prisons.

Many of the issues and disagreements across the three cultures—those of correctional officers, middle management, and administration—can be effectively addressed through consensus-building initiatives by correctional leaders. Part of visionary leadership is to build consensus, trust, and support among competing cultures within the organization. We address how consensus building can be achieved in prison organizations in Chapter 6 when we talk about transmitting and transforming correctional culture. For now, however, we need to briefly address what we believe are key or central correctional values: the relevance of vision for correctional leaders, and the significance of values and vision on correctional culture.

CORRECTIONAL VALUES AND VISION: THE IMPORTANCE OF CULTURE

What are the characteristics of an effective vision, and how is it related to leadership? Nanus (1992, p. 4) defines an effective leader in the following way:

> Effective leaders have agendas; they are totally results oriented. They adopt challenging new visions of what is both possible and desirable, communicating their visions, and persuade others to become so committed to these new directions that they are eager to lend their resources and energies to make them happen.

In other words, effective leaders are able to communicate to their employees their values and vision, and provide a road map on how to get to specific places that are desirable for the leader as well as the employees. Effective correctional leadership is not possible without thinking about organizational culture. Correctional leaders who develop agendas that are focused and result-oriented, and who communicate well to their employees and persuade them to head in the right direction, are really good leaders of culture.

Effective correctional leaders are able to comprehend major cultural values across the competing correctional cultures and meld them into one single vision for the organization. Through visionary practices, correctional leaders take the organization to places where they want it to be and reflect values that are important to correctional professionals and persons. So, what are the correctional values found within prison organizations among the competing cultures?

Earlier we discussed the idea of a unitary culture among correctional officers that stresses security and procustodial ideas among them, and we mentioned that this view may not actually reflect the cultural sentiments of many officers. In fact, correctional officers have a varied set of values that define their culture. Our review of the extant research showed that other values, such as human service work and the belief in professionalism, may be as important to the correctional officer culture as the values of custody and security.

The contrast offered by Johnson (1996, pp. 164–222) between public and private agendas of correctional officers might be a useful place to start in identifying the values among officers. An analysis of Johnson's ideas suggest that while bald, custodial values are espoused by many officers in their public and professional agenda, these same officers sometimes exhibit human service and helping values as part of their private agenda. Compelling evidence suggests that both sets of values define the correctional officer culture. This contrastive perspective recognizes the variability among officers concerning their values and expressions about their work. The correctional officer literature indicates that although many officers espouse values of security and safety in the prison, they also recognize human service work, compassion, and professionalism as equally compelling values and seek to express them in the work setting. Effective correctional leadership, therefore, must be cognizant of and willing to express these values in its correctional vision. To do otherwise serves to polarize and alienate correctional officers further from leaders and any vision the leaders might wish to express through the prison organization.

What about the values of middle managers in a correctional organization? For middle managers, the values of security and safety are as important as they are for correctional officers. Since many middle-management personnel come directly from rank-and-file correctional officer positions, it is not unusual that they identify with officer values. A stark contrast, however, lies in the fact that many middle-management positions are also considered first-line supervisory positions with the concomitant responsibilities of managing correctional officers. Therefore, middle managers have other values with which they are concerned. In effect, these middle managers are often stuck between two cultures: the officer culture on the one hand, and the management culture on the other. This can pose many difficulties for middle managers, and it is here that visionary leadership is the most critical.

Through visionary leadership, the officer culture and the middle-management culture can meet and forge an alliance to work toward realizing a particular vision supportive of specific values. For middle managers, values of efficiency, effectiveness, and consistency in practice tend to predominate. As managers, they have well-defined roles that require jobs to be done in specified ways, as indicated by policies and procedures. They are truly managers qua managers, and not necessarily leaders. They depend on the technical proficiency of the correctional staff and are concerned with accomplishing tasks, meeting deadlines, and making the sure the institution functions smoothly.

As a cultural group within the prison, middle managers have much to say about how the institution is run. Their allegiance to specific cultural values is both good and bad for the prison organization. On the one hand, the prison could never function without the vigilance of skilled managers; yet, on the other hand, an overemphasis on management concerns and values can drive an institution into the ground. This is where a correctional vision allows us to comprehend the forest from the trees within prisons. Although middle managers' strong cultural value of working within polices and procedures provides clear benefits to correctional organizations, much harm can be produced when existing policies, procedures, and practices actually work against an organization's mission or vision. In this way, a management value may be counterproductive to the long-term attainment of a correctional vision. In the words of Kevin Wright (1994), prisons require tightness as well as looseness in their operations. The management values of efficiency, stability, and predictability must be balanced with the competing values of flexibility, responsiveness, and creativity to allow a vision to take hold among correctional staff.

Correctional leaders who sit in positions of power must recognize the daily dilemmas and disjunctures found across the correctional officer and middle-management cultures. They, through a vision, must pull together the concerns of officers for safety and security, and the values of routine and stability that middle managers hold dear. These values are culturally based; they are rooted in deep-seated assumptions that both correctional cultures have about what the organization is doing and where it should be headed. The effective correctional leader taps into these values when developing a vision for the prison, in addition to being cognizant of environmental influences that will constrain and serve as a partial determinant of the correctional vision.

What about the top command culture of correctional leaders? This is the most important culture in the prison for two specific reasons: (1) these administrators are most subject to environmental influences, and (2) they are the people who set the moral tone of the organization. First and foremost, values of correctional leaders are determined, in part, by environmental influences. These influences include but are not limited to: politicians, legislatures, courts, professional associations, public expectations, economic and social conditions, unions, and the philosophy of executives such as governors. This is not to suggest that correctional leaders have no, or only a limited, input into their organizations, or that their personal and professional values are not important to developing and promoting a correctional vision. On the contrary, one of the most critical elements in the development of an effective correctional vision is how correctional leaders define their own values, along with how they practice them in the presence of their employees and how they communicate them both internally and externally to the prison.

So what are the values of top leaders within correctional organizations? First, given the constraints on their positions, many correctional leaders value positive relations with their environments. Most notable is their concern for what values are expressed by chief executives, usually a governor and/or a legislative committee. In addition, correctional leaders tend to value resources, both human and financial. They understand only too well that the public sector places, in the words of Lipsky (1980), infinite demands on agencies with limited, finite resources to achieve them, so correctional leaders put a high premium on obtaining and maintaining stable relations with key actors in the environment who can maximize their resources. Moreover, correctional leaders understand the importance of people to correctional work; they know correctional work is really people work, so many attempt to develop programs and efforts that put people first in the organization. Accentuating the positive aspects of people is critical to an effective correctional vision. As a value, nothing can be more relevant to the success or failure of a correctional vision than how it views people. Good correctional leaders understand that people are the essential element that defines the character of the organization and take great strides to incorporate their employees' values, as well as their own, into a comprehensive correctional vision.

In addition, the values of correctional leaders are crucial to the prison because they set the moral tone or sentiment for the organization. Leaders' values are critical to the success or failure of any correctional vision. If anyone in a correctional organization has the responsibility to define what is important, it must be the leaders. Correctional officers, prison staff, and middle managers are looking for, and in some cases begging for, correctional leaders to lead. Staff want to know what the leaders value and where the organization is headed; they seek out a vision statement that incorporates their concerns, as well as the concerns of others in the organization. Running in place too often has been the norm for prisons. In the absence of effective leadership, correctional staff are left to fend for themselves, and the competing cultures can clash and become counterproductive.

If the top leaders in correctional organizations do nothing else, they must state and express their values in a clear and concise manner. Effectively communication of their values and how they fit into a vision for the prison must be transmitted to employees. In Chapter 6, we will express this idea more directly. For now, we state the relevance of communicating values through a vision only to highlight how such a process influences the three cultures examined in this chapter. As a correctional leader, being able to state directly what one's values are and how they are consistent with the values of the other cultures within the correctional setting will do more to allow one to lead than just about anything else. Such expression of values through a vision defines the leader and where the leader wants to go. It is the first step in affecting the three cultures in such a way that a unifying culture is possible.

VISIONARY LEADERSHIP, CORRECTIONAL CULTURE, AND THE ENVIRONMENT: AN OPTIMISTIC VIEW

Correctional leaders cannot control everything that can possibly influence their organizations. As public employees, they are significantly influenced by the political process that defines their authority and determines their budgets. Nevertheless, correctional leaders can redefine themselves in such a way as to give them greater input over what happens to them. As stated earlier, too often correctional leaders have abdicated their proper leadership roles and slid back into being managers. We need good correctional managers, but we also need leaders who can direct, inspire, and align employees toward a correctional vision for the future.

DiIulio (1987) offers a similar view when he calls into question the usefulness of traditional sociological explanations of why prisons are unmanageable and suggests that prison managers have found such explanations administratively convenient to hide their own shortcomings. We agree with DiIulio at one level, yet we think his focus on management is misdirected. The real focus should be on leadership, and as we suggested in Chapter 1, leadership and management are not the same thing. The key point of contrast is that managers work within the parameters of the correctional vision created by leaders. Correctional leaders define the vision and, most importantly, work with the extant correctional cultures in their organizations to make the vision possible. It is through the leader's sense of vision, commitment, and values that correctional organizations can move forward into the future. Moreover, it is through leadership, not management, that people are willing to commit to a correctional vision.

This is why one cannot discuss leadership without examining how it influences the various cultures within correctional organizations. For the remainder of this book, we will describe the three cultures within prison organizations in more detail, and explain why leadership is so crucial is coalescing them toward a shared correctional vision. We place a high premium on correctional leadership and its role in influencing correctional cultures, yet at the same time, we recognize that correctional leadership is not the panacea for all the ills that face prison organizations. Governors, legislatures, and other interest groups have a significant say in how prisons are run, but these environmental entities also can be influenced by leaders. Our view is one of hope that correctional leaders can do more with less and lead more effectively in the 21st century.

In the next part of the book, we will more thoroughly describe the correctional cultures of officers, middle managers, and top command leaders. Our focus will be to show the diversity of values found both within and among the various correctional cultures. An understanding of these cultures will assist correctional leaders in defining a mission statement and a correctional vision. The next chapter will examine correctional officer culture in detail. Chapter 5 will extend the analysis to include middle managers and the top command culture and the relevance of a mission statement and vision to correctional organizations. Once these competing cultures are understood, we will, in Chapter 6, discuss ways in which these cultures can be unified, transmitted, and transformed to be consistent with a correctional vision.

CASE SCENARIO   *No Place for Social Workers*

Correctional officers on the Emergency Response Team (ERT) at Dixon Correctional Institution viewed themselves as somewhat of an elite group. Part of the reason for this view was that one had to *qualify* to be on the team. Members typically had to possess a clean record with no disciplinary write-ups or tardiness on their record and strong performance evaluations. In addition, the maximum security prison had a requirement of 80% accuracy in terms of shotgun and handgun proficiency for ERT certification. Moreover, the members had to demonstrate the ability to handle volatile situations and to step in as needed to assist coworkers.

In practice, the ERT had an esprit de corps and their own way of handling situations at the prison. They respected colleagues who showed gumption, those who weren't afraid to confront a risky situation. Inmates were collectively viewed as "scumbags" and not to be trusted. One of their key tenets was to subdue the inmate first and leave the questions for the treatment staff.

Mike Chambers volunteered for the ERT because of a desire to do something more challenging at the prison. He enjoyed working with inmates and believed that verbal de-escalation was the most important skill of an officer. Chambers actually enjoyed his weeks of training, since the training was very physical and exhilarating. He believed that the procedures he was learning were really "last-ditch" efforts at inmate compliance. His first encounter with the ERT was during training. He observed a strong camaraderie among ERT members. Their solidarity

was evident in their behavior, as well as their way of dress. Most came from military backgrounds and tended to have closely shaved heads. They also had nicknames for each other, such as "Kamikaze" and "Brutus," and socialized regularly after their shifts. He wondered how he would fit in with this tightly knit group.

The first emergency response call was exciting for Chambers. He could feel the adrenalin rush as he suited up with his coworkers. The situation called for the cell extraction of an inmate on Unit G. The inmate was familiar to Chambers from his work on several different units. He was rather surprised this particular inmate was causing trouble, since the inmate was known to be easygoing. At the doorway of the cell, Chambers started to speak to the inmate when another ERT member grabbed his arm and retorted sharply, "Forget that crap and let's just get him out."

Later, as the team was changing out of their gear, that same coworker admonished him for hesitating and "playing like a social worker." The other members laughed and told him that he wouldn't last long if he hesitated like that again in a risky situation. Several emergency response situations later, Chambers decided to resign from the team. While the others would aggressively respond to emergency situations, Chambers tended to hang back as he tried to assess the scope of the problem. He realized that he simply did not fit with this group. He did not share their assumptions about inmates or their desire to "kick butt."

Case Scenario continued

Case Scenario Questions

1. Do you recognize a subgroup at Dixon Correctional Institution? What are the characteristics of this subgroup? What are the group members' shared assumptions, and how do these assumptions affect their work performance?

2. Do you see any drawbacks to having a dominant subgroup among correctional officers at Dixon Correctional Institution? How does this subgroup relate to the subculture research in this chapter?

REFERENCES

Breed, A. F. (1998). Corrections: A victim of situational ethics. *Crime and Delinquency, 44*(1), 9–18.

Cheek, F., & Miller, D. (1982). Reducing staff and inmate stress. *Corrections Today, 44,* 73–78.

Cheek, F., and Miller, D. (1983). The experience of stress for corrections officers: A double-bind theory of correctional stress. *Journal of Criminal Justice, 11,* 105–120.

Clear, T., & Cole, G. (2000). *American corrections* (5th ed.). Belmont, CA: Wadsworth.

Crouch, B., & Marquart, J. (1983). On becoming a prison guard. In B. Crouch (Ed.), *The Keepers*. Springfield, IL: Charles C. Thomas.

DiIulio, J. (1987). Governing prisons: A comparative study of correctional management. New York: Free Press.

DiIulio, J. (1991). *No escape: The future of American corrections*. New York: Basic Books.

Farkas, M., Manning, P. K. (1997). The occupational cultures of policing and correctional work. *Journal of Crime and Justice, 22*(2), 51–68.

Houston, J. (1999). *Correctional management: Functions, skills, and systems* (2nd ed.). Chicago: Nelson-Hall.

Irwin, J., & Austin, J. (1997). *It's about time: America's imprisonment binge* (2nd ed.). Belmont, CA: Wadsworth.

Jacobs, J., & Retsky, H. (1980). Prison guard. In B. Crouch (Ed.), *The Keepers*. Springfield, IL: Charles C. Thomas.

Johnson, R. (1996). *Hard times: Understanding and reforming the prison* (2nd ed.). Belmont, CA: Wadsworth.

Johnson, R., & Price, S. (1981). The complete correctional officer human service and human environment of prison. *Criminal Justice and Behavior, 8,* 343–373.

Kauffman, K. (1988). *Prison officers and their world*. Cambridge, MA: Harvard University Press.

Klofas, J. (1984). Reconsidering prison personnel, new views of the correctional officer subculture. *International Journal of Offender Therapy and Comparative Criminology, 28,* 169–75.

Klofas, J., & Toch, H. (1982). The guard subculture. *Journal of Research in Crime and Delinquency, 19*(2), 238–54.

Lipsky, M. (1980). *Street-level bureaucracy.* New York: Russell Sage Foundation.

Lombardo, L. (1989). *Guards imprisoned.* Cincinnati, OH: Anderson.

Nanus, B. (1992). *Visionary leadership.* San Francisco: Jossey-Bass.

Owen, B. A. (1988). *The reproduction of social control: A study of prison workers at San Quentin.* New York: Praeger.

Poole, R., & Regoli, R. (1981). Alienation in prison. *Criminology, 19*(2), 251–70.

Schein, E. H. (1990). Organizational culture (the changing face and place of work). *The American Psychologist, 45,* 109–120.

Stojkovic, S., Kalinich, D., & Klofas, J. (1998). *Criminal justice organizations administration and management* (2nd ed.). Belmont, CA: West/Wadsworth.

Wright, K. (1994). *Effective prison leadership.* Binghamton, NY: William Neil.

Zimmer, L. (1986). *Women guarding men.* Chicago: University of Chicago Press.

two

CORRECTIONAL CULTURE: OFFICERS, MANAGERS, AND LEADERS

CORRECTIONAL OFFICERS AND THEIR CULTURE

The preceding chapter proposed a view of correctional work as a unitary culture. This chapter will adopt an integrative model of correctional culture, with the knowledge that many cultures exist within the correctional organization. It will then systematically describe the dimensions and focal concerns of these formal and informal cultures. The view that there are multiple subcultures in the hierarchy of the organization is presented. The purpose of the chapter is to provide students with a cultural understanding of correctional work and with an understanding of the differentiation within these cultures. Students will become aware of multiple cultures with differing values and concerns at all levels in the organizational hierarchy and then consider the implications for the organization and for correctional leadership.

THE FORMAL COMPONENT OF CORRECTIONS

The formal component of the correctional organization consists of its official mission and policies; the formal objectives in recruitment, selection, and training; the rank structure and hierarchical chain of command; and its union mandates. In corrections, this formal component has a corresponding culture with bureaucratic characteristics, strong militaristic overtones, and values of custody and control. The following sections describe these elements in greater detail.

The Official Mission

Most correctional organizations or programs have some form of overall mission or set of overriding principles. Stojkovic, Kalinich, and Klofas (1998) describe a mission as a statement or description of an organization's common purpose; continuing purpose for existing responsibility to its clients or constituents; and its ideology, values, and operating principles (p. 28). The mission describes the general direction of the overall organization in broad and long-range terms. Ideally the mission provides a clear understanding of the agency's purpose, goals, and objectives (Stojkovic et al., 1998). For example, the "protection of the public through the incarceration of offenders" and the "safe, secure and humane control of offenders" are common elements in the mission statements of many departments or divisions of corrections. These statements convey the message that custody and control are of paramount importance to the department of corrections and its employees. Less common are such mission statements as "providing offenders with opportunities to become productive, law-abiding citizens" and "providing humane and respectful treatment of offenders." These statements transmit the message that human service activities are valued as core responsibilities and tasks of the department and its employees.

The mission statement is very much influenced by the political ethos and agendas of particular groups external to the prison. The mission of the South Carolina Department of Corrections includes an assurance that crime victims will be treated with dignity, respect, and sensitivity. This is clearly an offering to victims' groups and advocates in the larger society. Likewise, a mission statement with an element of "public protection and secure control of offenders" is a response to the societal demands to "get tough" on crime promulgated by the media and legislatures.

Communication of the mission must infiltrate the policies, practices, and procedures of the organization. Problems with ineffective or convoluted messages or interruptions in the flow of communication may have several consequences for an organization. Correctional staff may not understand, accept, or value the goals and may even develop their own sentiments and norms that are incompatible with the official mission. They may reject the goals as being too lofty, inoperable, and inapplicable to their everyday routines and tasks. Correctional officers can do only what they believe is achievable. In the absence of effective communication, some officers may become completely aberrant, pursue their own agenda, and ignore the legitimate means (Stojkovic et al., 1998). Other officers may try to blend the official goals and imperatives with their own values and sentiments in order to find a more congruous work approach. An organizational mission emphasizing the custody and control of inmates and holding inmates accountable for their actions would be modified by such officers to include human service activities. In this manner, they would shape the mission to what they think it should be and work around the goals of the organization.

Most significant to this chapter is the importance of a clearly articulated mission statement in implementing policies, practices, and procedures, and ultimately, in achieving an understanding of and commitment to that mission on the part of correctional staff. Without this clarity in direction, organizational members may search for and develop their own ideas and values that are in direct opposition to the mission statement and goals. Ideally the mission is sparked by a vision of a specific organizational culture in the prison that values supervisory staff and employees and develops their potential to the fullest in carrying out their duties. Correctional employees will be inspired in their work responsibilities by such a vision from correctional leaders. This subject is explored more fully in the chapters that follow this one.

Recruitment, Selection, and Formal Training

Historically, departments and divisions of corrections have not been very aggressive or creative in the recruitment of correctional officers. Typically such methods as posters, job announcements, and Internet postings on their Web sites have been used. High turnover and problems with retention of officers have resulted in minimal standards set in order to fill numerous vacancies quickly (Stinchcomb & Fox, 1999). The minimal qualifications to become a correctional officer include: a minimum age of at least 18 or 21 years, a high school diploma or GED, and no felony convictions. Unfortunately, keeping the standards at a minimum results in a pool of minimally qualified candidates.

The selection process for applicants ideally would be designed to identify the most suitable candidates for the job, but in some instances, the pool of candidates has not been sizable enough to make that distinction. The most common screening instruments in the selection of correctional officers are the written civil service examination and the oral interview (Stinchcomb & Fox, 1999). Some states use psychological screening of all corrections officers in the hope of identifying highly unusual psychological profiles (Stojkovic et al., 1998). Assessment centers are also used in some departments of corrections. Candidates are subjected to exercises that test mental ability, and oral, written, and human relations skills (Champion, 1998).

An individual who becomes an officer undergoes a period of formal training. Whether this occurs before or after actual on-the-job training depends on the needs of the institution. This training period varies from state to state but is typically between five and nine weeks (Stinchcomb & Fox, 1999). Formal training is an important stage of occupational socialization, with exposure to both the formal and informal cultural values of the organization.

Concrete, practical knowledge to use in the supervision and management of inmates is emphasized in formal training. Officers learn the mechanical skills necessary for the job, such as incident and disciplinary report writing, cell extraction, restraint procedures, radio communication procedures and codes, and how to operate locks and keys. Recruits also attend classes on such topics as legal rights of officers and inmates, criminal thinking of inmates, and professionalism.

Interfaced with the formal training are small doses of the realities of correctional work by experienced officer trainers. These "war stories" serve as a prelude to the on-the-job training to follow and as an important socializing force to the informal officer culture. Recruits learn to respect and even to emulate the styles of veteran trainers who have "been there" and have "seen it all." These trainers then become recruits' reference group for what approach to use in managing inmates. The recruits learn the cultural values of correctional work. For example, officers are warned to keep a distance from inmates because they are manipulative and tricky; they are told to remain aloof and to watch out for the "con." Recruits also realize that technical skills and custodial responsibilities are a prime focus, since the training concentrates on these.

On-the-job training exposes new officers to the realities of correctional work. These officers initially view the more experienced officers on their posts as a point of reference, but this dissipates over time as they become accustomed to handling inmates on a daily basis. In time officers develop their own way of handling inmates, and one that is workable for them. Several factors shape these officers' outlooks. The presence of a predominant type of officer either on their particular unit or in the prison may influence their choice of style. In a prison with a tight-knit, dominant subculture of officers displaying a procustodial, anti-inmate, antimanagement orientation and values, newer officers may feel compelled to act accordingly in order to be accepted. The type of inmate under supervision is another influential factor in the choice of style. An officer who works on a specialized unit for elderly inmates may have a much different approach than one who works on a segregation unit with disturbed, disruptive inmates. The leadership in the prison, a central topic of this book, is still another significant variable affecting an officer's approach to working with inmates.

Rank Structure and Hierarchical Chain of Command

The formal culture of the correctional organization may be viewed as bureaucratic because of its heavy emphasis on formalized policy and procedure, documentation of any and all incidents and activities, and task specialization. It is also regarded as paramilitary because of its rank structure, clearly articulated chain of command, and military overtones in relations among members. The rank structure consists of line officers, sergeants, lieutenants, and captains.

Line officers hold the rank of sergeant or below (Correctional Officer I, II, or III). They may work on several different posts, with the majority of officers working on the inmate housing units. Task specialization is evident, as the duties and tasks are carefully defined in job descriptions for each post. Supervisory duties on the housing units include head counts, inmate escort to activities, periodic cell searches, general observation, periodic unit patrol, disciplinary write-ups, and report writing. Many officers view these posts as stressful, while others find them challenging (Farkas, 1999). Officers may adopt various approaches when working in direct and prolonged contact with inmates.

Subcultures of officers are engendered as officers realize they share values, attitudes, and sentiments far different from their colleagues and management. Some correctional officers strongly enforce any and all rules and adopt a tough exterior. They embrace custodial values and have a punitive attitude toward inmates. Other officers find their own way to circumvent the rules and to incorporate a human service approach. They have an interest in helping inmates and enjoy working closely with them. They also tend to coalesce, as Johnson (1996) maintains. This culture is more private, since the human service-oriented officers fear the ridicule or rejection of their custodial-oriented colleagues.

Other posts for officers in the lower ranks consist of tower and gatehouse posts. Officers stationed in the towers have very little direct contact with inmates or other officers during their shifts. The contact is limited to telephone or radio calls to the control center. The tower officers have as their primary responsibility the identification of potential escapes or disturbances by inmates. They usually have a firearm and must follow the use-of-force guidelines in their state for stopping an escape or ending a disturbance. Correctional officers who work the gatehouse posts are the "gatekeepers" for the institution. They check in inmate visitors, professional visitors, and staff. Their duties include logging visitors, processing them through the metal detector, searching belongings, and answering calls to the facility. They also "buzz" the visitors and staff through to the facility entrance once approved. Farkas (2000) found that officers who work these posts tend to be loners. They like the solitude of their post and prefer limited contact with inmates and fellow officers.

Correctional line officers may also supervise certain areas of the institution, including visiting and dining areas, workshops, recreation areas, and program locations. Because of the congregation of large groups of inmates, these posts require vigilance for contraband manufacture and exchange and other illegal behaviors. Sergeants supervise these areas, as well as the housing units. They ensure that posts are filled for officers on sick leave, disability leave, or vacation. They may even fill in on a vacant post.

Segregation is another post to which line officers may be assigned. This position involves working with some of the most difficult inmates at the prison. Some research shows that officers who work on segregation units hold more punitive views toward inmates and tend to express their authority more coercively (Farkas, 2000). It is not clear whether working on segregation units shapes the outlook of officers to a more punitive, anti-inmate perspective or whether a certain type of officer volunteers to work on those units. Nonetheless, officers who work on segregation units may form a subculture with a value system and a set of norms that differ sharply from the official mission and the values of colleagues on other units.

Middle management consists of lieutenants and captains. They may still hold the values of line officers, since they were once in the lower ranks themselves and are not very far removed from the daily routines and occurrences in prison. They regularly walk through the cell blocks or housing units, and they understand the realities of correctional work. Often they are summoned to make a final decision concerning a critical incident involving inmates or an inmate and an officer. Yet they must also identify with the values of management, since they now supervise and evaluate line staff. It is their duty to inspect all areas of the institution for orderliness and security and to oversee the correctional staff, making certain they fulfill their responsibilities.

Middle managers have a duty to strictly follow the policies and procedures of the institution. They may write up line officers for a rule violation or deviance from policy or procedure. They also have an eye for promotion, which prompts them to identify even more with the management culture. Captains are often more preoccupied with paperwork and administrative tasks than lieutenants and have less time to exercise personal supervision over a specific unit or area of the prison (Jacobs & Retsky, 1975). They manage to separate themselves from the line staff more easily than do the lieutenants. As mentioned earlier, however, middle management is often enmeshed between two cultures: the officer culture and the management culture.

This hierarchical ordering and rank structure orients correctional officers to their position in relation to the higher and lower levels of authority and power in the organization and may fragment the organization by rank. Lines of authority and, to some extent, the boundaries of that authority are established. A vertical, top-down channel of communication is also set in place by this hierarchy of authority. The foci and areas of responsibility are defined differently based on rank. Line officers believe that management cannot understand the realities of their work situation, since managers no longer work in direct, prolonged contact with inmates. In their view, management is there only to oversee them and to watch for mistakes. Supervisory staff believe that they do understand the work demands and responsibilities of line staff, but that they have earned their stripes and should be accorded respect for their achievement. They, too, see their role as primarily overseeing and evaluating line officers.

Correctional Work and Unions

Correctional officers in most states have the right to organize, and some 60% of officers do belong to a union (American Correctional Association, 1994). Unionism and the establishment of collective bargaining has had an enormous impact on the formal culture of correctional work. Organizational power in prison has been redistributed and an alternative basis for authority has been established in an organization that traditionally demanded single-minded allegiance to those in command (Jacobs & Retsky, 1975, p. 41).

The relations between management and correctional employees are increasingly defined by the labor contract. Collective bargaining has increased the formalization of personnel policies and procedures, increased job security, and reduced managerial discretion in matters of discipline and discharge, promotion, transfers, and work assignments (Katz & Kochan, 1992, p. 378). Most union contracts specify the number of hours employees can work in a specific pay period, restrict the transfer of correctional officers within a prison, and subject any employee disciplinary action to a specific set of procedures (Mays & Winfree, 1998). The rules in the labor contract have legal force because they are contractual and can be enforced in a court of law (Smith, 2000).

The positive aspect of unionism for employees is that major issues are brought to the fore for discussion and negotiation. The administration may have been formerly unaware of these matters of concern to correctional employees. Stinchcomb and Fox (1999) point to a change over the years in the issues of importance to employees. Today's correctional officers are more likely to fight for intrinsic issues surrounding job satisfaction, personal autonomy, job enrichment, and self-sufficiency, rather than the extrinsic matters of earlier years. The negative side of unionism is that contact between supervisors and employees has become depersonalized, and the power and discretion of supervisors in managing their employees have been reduced. Unionism may also serve to further divide line officers from supervisory staff. Correctional officers may feel that their concerns are not necessarily issues of concern to management. They may then develop a culture with their own rules of how do things and a normative code of conduct and a set of values that are incongruent with the official culture.

DIMENSIONS OF THE CORRECTIONAL OFFICER CULTURE

Danger and Uncertainty

Correctional work is at times routine and monotonous, and at other times risky and unpredictable (Farkas & Manning, 1997). Officers must remain in a constant state of alertness and readiness in the advent of trouble or danger. Several studies point to the danger and uncertainty of the job as a major impact on work-related stress (Triplett, Mullings, & Scarborough, 1996). Finn (1998) discusses several factors that have increased the danger of the job: inmate crowding and no corresponding increase in the number of supervisory staff, an increase in the number of inmate assaults on officers in state and federal institutions, and the introduction of more gang-affiliated inmates and more dangerous gangs. This perception of potential danger may affect the desire of officers to engage in human service delivery to inmates. Officers may cling to their custodial beliefs to mask the fear and uncertainty engendered by potentially dangerous interactions with inmates.

Establishing and Expressing Authority

Establishing and expressing authority with inmates varies by type of officer. Some correctional officers use exchange or negotiation, rather than coercion, as a base of authority. Carroll (1974) asserts that correctional officers cannot rely on force to achieve compliance because they are dealing with inmates who may be serving life terms, some with no possibility of parole. Hence the inmates are already punished to the limit and have little to lose. In addition, the use of force may provoke an answering response on the part of inmates, increasing the risk of danger or violence.

The use and effectiveness of coercive authority is also limited by social, legal, and institutional reforms (Carroll, 1974). Increased documentation, ombudsman and inmate grievance committees, as well as increased court scrutiny into prison conditions and the treatment of inmates have limited the use of coercion. Just as the power to punish has been curtailed, so has the power to reward. The formal reward system (e.g., good time, parole, and program participation) has been substantially affected by bureaucratic and judicial reforms that have eliminated officer influence in reward decisions. In addition, social reforms (in the form of counselors, therapists, and special committees) have reduced officer influence in decision making with respect to job and program assignments. The absence of access to the distribution of formal rewards has compelled officers to establish informal norms of reciprocity with inmates.

Dependency relationships form between officers and inmates as a means to keep order in the prison environment. Inmates depend on officers for protection from predatory inmates, assignments to housing and work areas, disciplinary actions, and for the allocation of a variety of goods and services. They also need officers to provide information about the organization, such as norms, procedures, and techniques. In turn, officers depend on inmates for their personal safety in a work situation with a high inmate-to-staff ratio. They may also need inmates to assist in the performance of some of their functions or duties (e.g., helping to keep order in the lunchroom).

Officers use informal rewards to shape and control the behavior of inmates. They may overlook minor rule infractions, exchange information, and grant special favors or privileges. In addition, guards have learned to rely on the utilization of interpersonal communication skills, such as persuasion and leadership. Use of these skills avoids the use of coercion and averts trouble. In the process of this exchange and negotiation, officers become human service providers. According to Hepburn (1984), the level of institutional authority is greatest among those officers who are less punitive and less custodial, and who maintain less social distance from inmates. These officers also express a higher level of job satisfaction. In other words, human service officers have more authority with inmates and are more satisfied with their jobs (Johnson, 1996).

Correctional Work as "People Work"

Correctional work is "people work," and its primary tools are the reading of human behavior, understanding of behavioral cues, and good judgment (Farkas, 1999). Correctional officers have the most direct and prolonged contact with inmates. Because of this, they have been referred to as "first-line treatment agents," in terms of diagnosing and referring troubled inmates (Poole & Regoli, 1981). Officers familiarize themselves with the inmates on their units or in their areas, and they are then sensitive to any changes in the behavior of a particular inmate. They are the first to notice atypical or abnormal behavior on the part of inmates and signs of decompensation in mentally ill inmates. They may routinely refer troubled inmates for psychological services and advise, console, or assist inmates with institutional adjustment problems. In order to carry out these varied responsibilities, officers need an understanding of human behavior and skills in interpersonal communication. It is these human relations skills that can be used to develop relationships, reduce tension, defuse crises, and conduct daily business in a civilized manner (Johnson, 1996).

Human service or people skills, however, are typically not recognized or rewarded by colleagues and supervisors. Performance evaluations, for example, center on the safety and orderliness of the unit rather than on how many inmates were referred for psychological evaluation. And colleagues may ridicule or even harass human service officers or "people workers" regarding their attitude and behavior toward inmates. The officers with core values of human service may then gravitate toward colleagues who share their belief in providing a range of services to susceptible inmates (Johnson, 1979, p. 155).

Orientation and Relations with Inmates

Attitudes toward inmates vary among correctional officers. Researchers have tried to identify personal and organizational factors as sources of these attitudes. The majority of studies have shown that the age of the officer makes a difference. Older correctional officers generally have a more favorable orientation toward inmates (Jacobs & Kraft, 1978; Jurik, 1985) and are less punitive (Klofas, 1986; Farkas, 1999). Most studies have found no association between gender and officer attitude; however, Zimmer (1986) found that women adopt their specific work approach based on their attitude toward working with inmates. Female officers in the "inventive role," for example, choose this style because they like the challenge of working closely with inmates. Recent studies have also found race to be related to the orientation of officers. Black officers hold more positive attitudes toward inmates and the rehabilitative potential of inmates (Jackson & Ammen, 1996; Van Voorhis, Cullen, Link, & Wolfe, 1991).

Organizational factors affecting officers' attitudes toward inmates have also been explored. Among the significant variables were seniority, role conflict, and job satisfaction. More experienced officers have more positive attitudes toward inmates and are more rehabilitative in their outlook (Farkas, 1999; Klofas & Toch, 1982). Officers with high role conflict have a more punitive orientation toward inmates (Cullen, Lutze, Link, & Wolfe, 1989; Hepburn & Albonetti, 1980; Poole & Regoli, 1980). Correctional officers with a human service orientation are more satisfied with their jobs (Hepburn & Knepper, 1993).

Officer relations with inmates is another area of interest to correctional administrators. Solving inmate problems often becomes a routine task for officers. Requests for cell changes, concern over threats from other inmates, and difficulties adjusting to prison are a few of the daily inmate issues that officers confront. This problem-solving role requires personalized relations with inmates; however, even while officers try to help inmates and maintain good rapport or good working relationships with them, they must be alert to the possibility of being manipulated or taken advantage of by inmates. There is always the potential for confrontation and violence when working in close proximity to inmates. This is a population of human beings held against their will, and as such, they may be expected to be resistive to correctional authority.

Yet those officers who do acknowledge their problem-solving duties have discovered the positive consequences. In the process of helping inmates, they have gained more control over their work environment, more security in their daily interactions with inmates, and a sense of community with inmates under their care (Johnson, 1996, p. 242). Respect for one's humanity matters enormously to inmates, and they reciprocate by treating officers with respect and consideration (Johnson, 1996).

Relations with Coworkers

Peer support is critical to the adjustment and attachment of correctional officers to the organization. Research generally points to a lack of cohesion among officers. Poole and Regoli (1981) contend that the development of extensive camaraderie and in-group solidarity is inhibited by the minimal interaction with coworkers (i.e., at shift end or staffings) and the expectation that officers perform their tasks alone. In addition, the increasing diversity of the officer force with the integration of minorities and women has fragmented the once largely white, male ranks. The high turnover among correctional officers also affects cohesiveness.

Several studies have suggested that officers do, indeed, feel alienated from their coworkers, yet they still adhere to a normative code of behavior toward one another (Farkas, 1997; Kauffman, 1988). Peer group pressure to conform to existing attitudes, values, and beliefs about inmates and the job adds stress, particularly for newer officers. Officers may feel inwardly that they should be professional and assist inmates in their adjustment and coping in prison, but outwardly they must act hard and cold to appease their coworkers. Several studies have identified peer support as positively related to work stress (Cullen, Link, Wolfe, & Frank, 1985; Grossi & Berg, 1991); in other words, interactions with coworkers actually heightened correctional officer stress.

Relations with Management

Relations with management are also problematic. Conflicts with management are a commonly reported source of stress or difficulty in studies of correctional officers (Veneziano, 1984). Toch and Klofas (1982) surmise that officers generally feel that they are autocratically managed and that their contributions are seldom solicited. Promotional policies of supervisory staff are a prime example. Officers characterize these policies as arbitrary and based on favoritism (Jacobs & Retsky, 1977; Veneziano, 1984). The unclear performance guidelines of supervisory staff contribute to a confusion regarding promotional expectations. Officers are uncertain about exactly what they are evaluated on. If they enforce all the rules all of the time, they run the risk of being criticized for their inflexibility or punitiveness; yet if they exercise too much discretion and are flexible in rule enforcement, they risk being considered too easy, too weak, or ineffective.

Moreover, an overall lack of administrative support and a lack of input into decision making are major difficulties associated with managerial practices (Duffee, 1975; Lasky, Gordon, & Strebalus, 1986; Slate & Vogel, 1997; Veneziano, 1984). This lack of participation in decisions regarding policy issues that impact the officers' work environment increases occupational stress and thoughts about quitting (Slate & Vogel, 1997). Correctional officers complain of the insolence of inmates who feel free to disrespect officers and contradict orders because they view the officers as powerless to do anything about it (Duffee, 1975). Supervisors also fail to communicate policies to all staff members and provide direction to staff (Cheek & Miller, 1983; Lombardo, 1989).

CORRECTIONAL OFFICERS: FOCAL CONCERNS

Role Conflict, Role Ambiguity

Role conflict has received much attention as a significant source of stress for correctional officers. It may be defined as a conflict between the worker's expectations and the demands of the job. It is a result of ambiguous definitions that do not clarify which specific institutional goal workers should emphasize in the performance of their duties (Pogrebin & Atkins, 1982, p. 27). Role conflict also results from officers' perception that administrators desire only proper security, while officers wish to perform helping functions as well (Lombardo, 1989, p. 162). Most correctional institutions have a dual emphasis on custody and treatment, combining elements of both to a greater or lesser degree (Hepburn & Albonetti, 1980, p. 447). The institutional goal of maintaining order and security dictates that the correctional officer enforce rules and regulations, maintain order, and follow procedures and policies. The goal of treatment and rehabilitation mandates a more supportive, therapeutic manner of officer contact. Hepburn and Albonetti (1980) view these goals as divergent and mutually incompatible, resulting in the absence of clear role expectations or standards by which performance is to be evaluated.

Related to role conflict is role ambiguity. This is a consequence of the discrepancy in information available to workers on what is required for the adequate performance of their role (Kahn, Wolfe, Quinn, & Snoek, 1981). Restrictive or convoluted channels of communication in the hierarchical chain of command in an organization may result in role ambiguity. Correctional officers are charged with certain responsibilities and are expected to go "by the book," yet officers know they must use their own judgment to carry out these duties. In order to do this, all workers must have all the information relevant to their decisions and actions. Officers must know the scope of their responsibilities, the amount of their authority, and what criteria they will be evaluated on. Without this information, officers face uncertainty about which course of action to take and may revert to a custodial and security role because this is the only role on which they can be objectively evaluated (Jacobs & Retsky, 1975). Clearly, officers must find a workable middle ground between being too rigid or too lenient in enforcing and following rules (Finn, 1998).

Role conflict and role ambiguity may lead to greater job stress and a feeling of alienation and lack of commitment to the organization and other members of the organization. This stress affects the officer's ability to formulate an effective work ideology (Pogrebin & Atkins, 1982). No clearly stated guidelines for priority are communicated to officers, and therefore, they must act arbitrarily in translating the objectives into action (Pogrebin, 1980, p. 342). However, one study by Finn (1998) did find that the addition of a rehabilitative mission to the custodial function of correctional officers was "reinvigorating," and not a source of role conflict.

That correctional officers are experiencing a high degree of role conflict and role ambiguity is a concern for correctional leaders. Officers are receiving conflicting and confusing messages concerning the mission and goals of the organization. The leader's role is to create a culture with a clear mission that all members of the organization understand and are committed to. Officers must also understand what their duties are and the parameters of those duties within the organizational mission. The mission and goals should permeate the policies, practices, and procedures of the institution.

Job Stress

Individuals who work in correctional institutions experience a significant amount of stress in their job (Brodsky, 1977, 1982; Cheek & Miller, 1983). For purposes of this discussion, stress will be defined as a physiological, psychological, and social effect that is a perceived result of work conditions or the work environment. Stress is engendered by aversive events termed "stressors," and these stressors result in harmful or undesirable outcomes (Veneziano, 1984). Brodsky (1982) identifies three types of occupational stress: short-term, acute stress; stress of a time-bound event; and long-term, chronic stress. For correctional officers, short-term, acute stress is caused by a situation of unanticipated risk or danger, such as an inmate suddenly brandishing a weapon. Stress of a time-bound event is an anticipated stress that ends after completion of the event—the relief following a successful inspection by the warden, for example. Long-term, chronic stress is stress that a correctional officer must contend with over time. Although officers may experience all three forms at various points in their career, chronic stress is most often reported in studies on correctional officers (Brodsky, 1977, 1982), and it is this stress that causes physiological and psychological symptoms and social dysfunction.

Factors and conditions associated with work stress can be broadly categorized as personal and organizational. Among personal variables, the correlation between age, race and ethnicity, and education remains unclear. The evidence is stronger concerning gender and work stress. Research indicates that the pressures and stresses of correctional work may be enhanced for women (Cullen et al., 1985). Female correctional officers experience a gender-based form of stress not experienced by their male counterparts. Zimmer (1986) discusses the sex discrimination and sexual harassment confronted by female officers compounded by a lack of intervention and support by supervisors. Male coworkers are a strong source of opposition, along with male supervisors and male inmates. Work difficulties center around a feeling of having to always prove oneself able to perform the job on an equal basis with men.

Overall work-related variables rather than individual characteristics are more significant in understanding the stress of correctional work. The nature of the work and the perceived danger and unpredictability of working with inmates have been major sources of stress reported by officers (Launay & Fielding, 1989; Lombardo, 1989; Triplett, Mullings, & Scarborough, 1996). The high inmate-to-staff ratio and the increasingly violent, often gang-affiliated inmate population may exacerbate this feeling. Understaffing results in not enough time to get the job done and the need for officers to work overtime when scheduled staff does not show. Officers may experience fear and anxiety but are also under pressure not to show those feelings, lest their peers think them weak. They must appear strong and tough and able to handle any situation that arises. Working in a maximum security prison has been shown to be more stressful because of the more dangerous inmates, stricter rule enforcement, and pressure to show that officers can "handle inmates" (Cullen et al., 1985), although some research has found high stress across security levels (Lasky, Gordon, & Strebalus, 1986).

Administrative policies and procedures and supervisory practices have been identified as stressors for officers, specifically a lack of clear guidelines and lack of autonomy (Cheek & Miller, 1983; Lindquist & Whitehead, 1986). Supervisory demands to get the job done, rotating shifts, and third-shift work wreak havoc with family lives and reduce officers' ability to perform their duties because of fatigue (Finn, 1999).

The personal costs of stress for correctional officers are evident in the manifestation of physical problems, psychological problems, and social dysfunctions. Wayne (1977) found a higher rate of heart attacks among correctional officers than among other state workers. Occurrences of high blood pressure, heart disease, ulcers, and severe migraines were found in one study of correctional officers (Cheek and Miller, 1983). These officers were medicated and under doctors' care for these ailments. In addition, the authors reported that more than one third of officers were affected by irritability, frequent colds, excessive eating or loss of appetite, difficulty going to sleep or staying asleep, and being fidgety or tense.

A greater use of sick leave and a greater number of stress-related illnesses, including migraines, high blood pressure, and gastrointestinal disorders, have been reported among correctional officers as compared to most other state occupations, including policing (Honnold & Stinchcomb, 1985). Greater levels of psychological distress also have been found among officers (Lasky, Gordon, & Strebalus, 1986). Stress may be exhibited in the social relations of correctional officers. This occupational group reports high rates of divorce and marital difficulties (Cheek & Miller, 1983; Veneziano, 1984).

Job stress can be quite costly to the organization in terms of decreased productivity, employee turnover, health care, disability payments, sick leave, and absenteeism (Slate & Vogel, 1997). Prolonged stress has been shown to decrease physical stamina, mental alertness, and reaction time (Davidson & Cooper, 1981, p. 573). The work behavior of officers is affected by stress, and this may have drastic consequences in an occupation dependant on alertness and controlled responses. Stressed officers may become distracted or disinterested in their work activities, resulting in careless head counts of inmates and sloppy cell searches (Finn, 1999). Their ability to resolve potentially volatile situations is also impaired when they are irritable and tense. Extreme job stress among correctional officers can lead to burnout (Lindquist & Whitehead, 1986).

Correctional officers have few or no coping mechanisms to rely on in stressful situations or when feeling stressed. The formal culture of corrections emphasizes an impersonal bureaucratic approach to the job, while the informal culture values toughness and control in the face of confrontation and adversity. Thus officers tend to deny the stresses of their job and present a tough, macho image (Cheek & Miller, 1983; Veneziano, 1984). This denial prevents them from seeking help or becoming involved in stress reduction strategies. Correctional leaders must be aware of employee stress and the sources of that stress. They must work with officers to engender a culture in which officers feel free to discuss work stress with management and to collaboratively search for strategies to reduce stress.

Job Satisfaction and Motivational Issues

The job satisfaction of correctional officers is a significant issue for all members of the organization. For purposes of this discussion, job satisfaction is defined as "an overall affective orientation on the part of workers toward their job" (Kalleburg, 1977, p. 128). Since work is a primary activity in officers' lives, their physical and mental health are affected by the degree of satisfaction with their job. Negative attitudes toward colleagues, supervisors, inmates, or even the organization itself may result from a state of unhappiness or dissatisfaction with the job. In addition, this dissatisfaction may affect worker productivity and effectiveness in working with inmates.

These concerns have stimulated research into the determinants of job satisfaction and what aspects of correctional work provide the most satisfaction for officers. Personal factors have been explored to determine whether individuals evaluate job aspects differently based on race, gender, education, and age. Studies have shown that older officers are more satisfied with their work (Hepburn & Knepper, 1993; Rogers, 1991). Correctional officers with more education and experience have expressed greater job satisfaction (Cullen, Link, Wolfe, & Frank, 1985; Jurik & Halemba, 1984; Jurik & Musheno, 1986; Walters, 1996).

Structural explanations for job satisfaction also have been examined. As with job stress, work variables have a strong association with the job satisfaction of correctional officers. The intrinsic aspects of the job, which include aspects associated with the job itself, have been strongly associated with job satisfaction. Increased organizational support has been a major satisfying aspect of the work identified in the research (Cullen, Link, Wolfe, & Frank, 1985; Grossi, Keil, & Vito, 1996; Hepburn & Knepper, 1993). Wright, Saylor, Gilman, and Camp (1997) indicated that greater participation in decision making and increased job autonomy enhanced workers' occupational outcomes, leading to elevated commitment to the institution, higher job satisfaction, greater efficacy in working with inmates, and less job-related stress. A majority of studies have found a link between job satisfaction and a human service orientation (Farkas, 1999; Hepburn & Knepper, 1993; Johnson, 1996; Toch & Klofas, 1982; Lombardo, 1989). Correctional officers who emphasize human service delivery tend to cope better with stress and are more satisfied with their tasks (Cullen, Link, Wolfe, & Frank, 1985).

Yet some studies cite extrinsic factors such as compensation, job security, and benefits as explanations for job satisfaction. Some officers identify these factors as the most satisfying aspects of correctional work, rather than the challenge of the job or the chance to help inmates (Farkas, 1999; Lindquist & Whitehead, 1986; Lombardo, 1989). Role conflict and the stressful aspects of the job may combine to negatively affect satisfaction with the work itself, so officers find solace in the extrinsic factors. If intrinsic job satisfaction, that is, satisfaction with the work itself, is to be maximized, then the job must provide sufficient variety, sufficient complexity, sufficient challenge, and sufficient skill (Katz, 1964). Correctional leaders need to create a culture that values its employees and the various skills they bring to the job. Including human service tasks in correctional responsibilities and valuing these activities would be one strategy for increasing the intrinsic job satisfaction of correctional officers.

Employee Turnover—Problems with Retention

Turnover generally refers to employees who leave their jobs voluntarily through a disciplinary process or by their own volition. The loss of large numbers of correctional officers is certainly an issue that deserves attention, but traditionally it has received little attention from administrators. High turnover seems to have become part of the correctional culture without much thought being given to how qualified employees can be retained. Turnover rates vary in prisons across the country, from as low as 1% to as high as 45%, with an average rate of 17% (McShane, Williams, Shichor, & McClain, 1991).

Work situations in corrections generally do not allow employees to completely utilize the full range of their talents (Wright, 1993). Jurik and Winn (1987) found the correctional work environment to be the strongest predictor of turnover; the most important dimension distinguishing continuing officers from turnovers was their satisfaction with the intrinsic working conditions, including autonomy, authority, and perceived variety of tasks. Terminating officers are less satisfied with opportunities for input into organizational policies. The level of employee utilization has been related to subsequent turnover (Wright, 1991). Correctional officers who feel that their abilities are not being utilized are more likely to leave. In Wright's (1991) study, employees with the highest performance rating of "excellent" subsequently left their job. Reward systems in many correctional organizations do not promote retention of the more proficient employees because there are no formal procedures in place to reward the better performers (Wright, 1991).

Diversity in the workplace may be another issue related to turnover. Some studies have found race to be an issue of concern with employee turnover. Black officers hold more negative views of their supervisors (Jurik & Winn, 1987) and are more likely to terminate because of conflicts with predominantly white supervisors (Jacobs & Grear, 1977).

Roseman (1981) asserts that turnover has certain costs and benefits that must be considered. On the benefit side, turnover may infuse the organization with the vitality of new hires, new ideas, and fresh approaches. It also rids the organization of employees who do not fit and are not committed to organizational goals. The final benefit is that it encourages management to reexamine the organizational structure and the content of jobs in order to understand the reasons for the turnover. The costs of turnover are both tangible and intangible. Turnover has a monetary cost in the form of expenditures for recruitment, selection (interviews and testing), orientation and training, and separation of employees (particularly long-term employees). The intangible costs are also significant. Work demands increase as a result of the vacancies, and a loss of morale may occur. Employees may identify with the exiting employees and their reasons for leaving, which may stimulate additional turnover.

Thus, correctional leaders must do more than simply hire aggregates of people and warehouse them to fill slots vacant from employee attrition. Correctional leaders must try to improve the retention rate of officers. One place to start is in the work environment, since this has been identified as a primary factor affecting turnover. Correctional leaders must work to understand the culture of their institution and, in some cases, work to transform the culture to one that is tolerant of diversity and rewards and challenges employees to use their talents to the fullest. This is the subject of the final chapters of this text.

This chapter has attempted to characterize the formal and informal cultures of corrections. It has explored the dimensions and focal concerns in these cultures in order to highlight the major issues confronting correctional leaders. The next chapter will focus on the dimensions of culture expressed by administrators. The final chapters will discuss ways to transmit cultural values and beliefs to employees and to coalesce differing ideas, interests, and individuals into a congruent work group.

CASE SCENARIO   *Correctional Officers' Relations with Inmates*

Mary Wallis was excited about starting her new job as a correctional officer. After working at a variety of jobs from waitressing to factory work, corrections sounded like a more stable job situation and one that would be interesting. Mary enjoyed working with people and thought correctional work would give her the opportunity to use her interpersonal skills. On her first day, Mary was informed she would start on the Blue Housing Unit, a general housing unit for male inmates. Her academy training was scheduled in two months. She was a little uncomfortable starting the job without any formal training, but was determined to watch and learn from the other officers.

Mary's coworker on the unit was a rather talkative, brash male officer named Bart who had worked in corrections for 15 years. He told her not to worry about her lack of academy training and said he would teach her "all you need to know." Mary quickly learned the routines of head counts, report writing, and patrolling the unit. At first Bart would do most of the patrolling, but once he saw that she could handle herself and wasn't afraid of the inmates, he let her do more of it. She actually liked walking in the unit and getting to know the names and faces of the different inmates. She made it a point to never forget a name and to greet the inmates. Bart chastised her for this. He repeatedly warned her that she was getting too friendly with the inmates and that she would get "burned."

One day an inmate came up to her and asked her to change the channel on the TV. He said the program was boring and the inmates wanted to watch a movie on a different channel. Mary was busy writing a report so she gave the inmate the remote control and told him to bring it right back. She looked up a few seconds later to see two inmates in a pushing and shoving match by the TV area. She called to Bart, who was doing a cell check, and he ran down the stairs to the inmates.

"What are you two a——— doing?" he barked, as he pushed the inmates apart.

"She gave him the thing and I want to change the channel!" retorted one of the inmates.

"Give me the remote control, *now,* you idiot—you know the rules!" yelled Bart.

"But she gave me the thing!" insisted the inmate.

"I don't give a damn. Hand it over—*now!*" said Bart, raising his voice even further.

The inmate glared at Bart, and then at Mary. He hesitated, and then started to turn away.

"Don't even think it, unless you want to sit in seg for three days," warned Bart.

The inmate handed the remote control to Bart, muttering under his breath. Bart turned to Mary and said, "Don't you have any brains in your head at all? These guys are scumbags who will try to con you out of anything. You almost started a riot over a stupid remote control. *We* control what they watch, not *them.* You had better learn who the boss is."

Mary could feel the tears pricking her eyes as she said, "But you never told me about the remote control."

"Do I have to tell you every rule—didn't you read the rule book? *Read it*—from cover to cover!" Bart walked away, shaking his head.

Later, as they were in the locker room preparing to go home, Bart recounted the whole incident to his buddies. They laughed loudly and began to tease her about being "Mother Mary."

(continued)

Case Scenario continued

She tried to ignore them. Bart and his friends usually went out to eat after work, but they never asked Mary to go along. In a way she was glad, since she didn't like the way they talked about inmates. She put her things in her duffle bag and made her way slowly out the door. She asked herself why she ever thought this would be an interesting job.

Case Scenario Questions

1. How would you characterize Bart's approach to working with inmates? How about Mary's approach?

2. How would you characterize relations between Mary and her coworker(s)? Is there any way they could be improved?

REFERENCES

American Correctional Association. (1994). *Vital statistics*. Laurel, MD: Author.

Brodsky, C. M. (1977). Long-term stress in teachers and prison guards. *Journal of Occupational Medicine, 19*(2), 133–138.

Brodsky, C. M. (1982). Work stress in correctional institutions. *Journal of Prison and Jail Health, 2*(2), 74–102.

Carroll, L. (1974). *Hacks, blacks, and cons*. Lexington, MA: Lexington.

Champion, D. (1998). *Corrections in the United States. A contemporary perspective*. Englewood Cliffs, NJ: Prentice-Hall.

Cheek, F., & Miller, D. (1982). Reducing staff and inmate stress. *Corrections Today, 44,* 73–78.

Cheek, F., & Miller, D. (1983). The experience of stress for corrections officers: A double-bind theory of correctional stress. *Journal of Criminal Justice, 11,* 105–120.

Cullen, F. T., Link, B. G., Wolfe, N. T., & Frank, J. (1985). The social dimensions of correctional officer stress. *Justice Quarterly, 2*(4), 505–533.

Cullen, F. T., Lutze, F. E., Link, B.G., and Wolfe, N. T. (1989). The correctional orientation of prison guards: Do officers support rehabilitation? *Federal Probation, 53,* 33–42.

Davidson, M., & Cooper, C. L. (1981). A model of occupational stress. *Journal of Occupational Medicine, 23*(8), 564–574.

Duffee, D. (1975). *Correctional policy and prison organization*. New York: Halsted Press.

Farkas, M. A. (1997). The normative code among correctional officers: An exploration of components and functions. *Journal of Crime and Justice, 20*(1), 23–36.

Farkas, M. A. (1999). Correctional officer attitudes toward inmates and working with inmates in a "get tough" era. *Journal of Criminal Justice, 27*(6), 495–506.

Farkas, M. A. (2000). A typology of correctional officers. *International Journal of Offender Therapy and Comparative Criminology, 44*(4), 431–447.

Farkas, M. A. & Manning, P. K. (1997). The occupational cultures of corrections and police officers. *Journal of Crime and Justice, 20*(2), 51–68.

Finn, P. (1999). Correctional officer stress: A cause for concern and additional help. *Federal Probation, 62*(2), 65–74.

Grossi, E. L., & Berg, B. L. (1991). Stress and job dissatisfaction among correctional officers: An unexpected finding. *International Journal of Offender Therapy and Comparative Criminology, 35*(1), 73–81.

Grossi, E. L., Keil, T. J., & Vito, G. F. (1996). Surviving the joint? Mitigating factors of correctional officer stress. *Journal of Crime and Justice, 19*(2), 103–120.

Hepburn, J. R. (1984). The erosion of authority and the perceived legitimacy of inmate social protest: A study of prison guards. *Journal of Criminal Justice, 12*(6), 579–590.

Hepburn, J. R., & Albonetti, C. (1980). Role conflict in correctional institutions. *Criminology, 17*(4), 445–459.

Hepburn, J. R., & Knepper, P. (1993). Correctional officers as human service workers: The effect on job satisfaction. *Justice Quarterly, 10*(2), 315–335.

Honnold, J., & Stinchcomb, J. (1985, December). Officer stress: Costs, causes, and cures. *Corrections Today,* 46–51.

Jackson, J. S., & Ammen, S. (1996). Race and correctional officers' punitive attitude toward treatment programs for inmates. *Journal of Criminal Justice, 24*(2), 153–166.

Jacobs, J. B., & Grear, M. (1977). Dropouts and rejects: An analysis of the prison guard's revolving door. *Criminal Justice Review, 2*(2), 57–70.

Jacobs, J. B., & Kraft, L. (1978). Integrating the keepers: A comparison of African American and Caucasian prison guards. *Social Problems, 25,* 304–318.

Jacobs, J. B., & Retsky, H. C. (1975). Prison Guard. *Urban Life, 4*(1), 5–19.

Johnson, R. (1979). Informal helping networks in prison: The shape of grass-roots correctional intervention. *Journal of Criminal Justice, 7,* 53–70.

Johnson, R. (1996). *Hard times. Understanding and reforming the prison* (2nd ed.). Belmont, CA: Wadsworth.

Johnson, R., & Price, S. (1981). The complete correctional officer: Human service and the human environment of the prison. *Criminal Justice and Behavior, 8*(3), 343–373.

Jurik, N. (1985). Individual and organizational determinants of correctional officer attitudes toward inmates. *Criminology, 23*(3), 523–539.

Jurik, N., & Halemba, G. J. (1984). Gender, working conditions, and the job satisfaction of women in a non-traditional occupation: Female correctional officers in men's prisons. *Sociological Quarterly, 25,* 551–566.

Jurik, N., & Musheno, M. C. (1986). "The internal crisis of corrections: Professionalization and the work environment. *Justice Quarterly, 3,* 457–480.

Jurik, N., & Winn, R. (1987). Describing correctional security dropouts and rejects: An individual or organizational profile? *Criminal Justice and Behavior, 14*(1), 5–25.

Kahn, R. L., Wolfe, D. M., Quinn, R. P., & Snoek, J. D. (1981). *Organizational stress: Studies in role conflict and ambiguity.* Malabar, FL: Robert E. Krieger.

Kalleburg, A. L. (1977). Work values and job rewards: A theory of job satisfaction. *American Sociological Review, 42,* 124–143.

Katz, D. The motivational basis of organizational behavior. *Behavioral Science, 9,* 131–146.

Katz, H. C., & Kochan, T. A. (1992). *Introduction to collective bargaining and industrial relations.* New York: McGraw-Hill.

Kauffman, K. (1988). *Prison officers and their world.* Cambridge, MA: Harvard University Press.

Klofas, J. (1986). Discretion among correctional officers: The influence of urbanization, age and race. *International Journal of Offender Therapy and Comparative Criminology, 30*(2), 111–124.

Klofas, J., & Toch, H. (1982). The guard subculture myth. *Journal of Research in Crime and Delinquency, 19,* 169–175.

Lasky, G., Gordon, B., & Strebalus, D. J. (1986). Occupational stressors among federal correctional officers working in different security levels. *Criminal Justice and Behavior, 13*(3), 317–327.

Launay, G., & Fielding, P. J. (1989). Stress among prison officers: Some empirical evidence based on self report. *The Howard Journal, 28*(2), 138–147.

Lindquist, C., & Whitehead, J. (1986). Burnout, job stress, and job satisfaction among southern correctional officers: Perceptions and causal factors. *Journal of Offender Counseling, Services, and Rehabilitation, 10*(4), 5–25.

Lombardo, L. (1989). *Guards imprisoned.* (2nd ed.). Cincinnati, OH: Anderson.

Mays, G. L., & Winfree, L. T., Jr. (1998). *Contemporary corrections.* Belmont, CA: Wadsworth.

McShane, M., Williams, F., Shichor, D., & McClain, K. (1991). Examining employee turnover. *Corrections Today,* 220–225.

Pogrebin, M. (1980). Challenge to authority for correctional officers: A conflicting dilemma. *Journal of Offender Counseling, Services, and Rehabilitation, 4*(4), 337–342.

Pogrebin, M., & Atkins, B. (1982). Organizational conflict in correctional institutions. *Journal of Offender Counseling, Services, and Rehabilitation, 7*(1), 23–31.

Poole, E., & Regoli, R. (1980). Examining the impact of professionalism on cynicism, role conflict and work alienation among prison guards. *Criminal Justice Review, 5,* 57–65.

Poole, E., & Regoli, R. (1981). Alienation in prison. *Criminology, 19*(2), 251–270.

Rogers, R. (1991). The effects of educational level on correctional officers' job satisfaction. *Journal of Criminal Justice, 19,* 123–137.

Roseman, E. (1981). *Managing employee turnover.* New York: Amacon.

Slate, R. N., & Vogel, R. E. (1997). Participative management and correctional personnel: A study of the perceived atmosphere for participation in correctional decision making and its impact on employee stress and thoughts about quitting. *Journal of Criminal Justice, 25*(5), 397–408.

Smith, C. E. (1999). *Law and contemporary corrections*. Belmont, CA: Wadsworth.

Stinchcomb, J. B., & Fox, V. B. (1999). *Introduction to corrections*. Englewood Cliffs, NJ: Prentice-Hall.

Stojkovic, S., Kalinich, D., & Klofas, J. (1998). *Criminal justice organizations* (2nd edition). Belmont, CA: Wadsworth.

Toch, H., & Klofas, J. (1982). Alienation and desire for job enrichment among correctional officers. *Federal Probation, 46,* 35–47.

Triplett, R., Mullings, J. L., & Scarborough, K. E. (1996). Work-related stress and coping among correctional officers: Implications from organizational literature. *Journal of Criminal Justice, 24*(4), 291–308.

Van Voorhis, P., Cullen, F. T., Link, B. G., & Wolfe, N. T. (1991). The impact of race and gender on correctional officer's orientation to the integrated environment. *Journal of Research in Crime and Delinquency, 28,* 472–500.

Veneziano, C. (1984). Occupational stress and the line correctional officer. *Southern Journal of Criminal Justice, 8,* 214–231.

Walters, S. (1996). The determinants of job satisfaction among Canadian and American correctional officers. *Journal of Crime and Justice, 19*(2), 145–158.

Wright, T. A. (1991). The level of employee utilization and its effect on subsequent turnover. *The Journal of Applied Business Research, 7,* 25–29.

Wright, T. A. (1993). Correctional employee turnover: A longitudinal study. *Journal of Criminal Justice, 21,* 131–142.

Wright, R., Saylor, W., Gilman, E., & Camp, S. (1997). Job control and occupational outcomes among prison workers. *Justice Quarterly, 14*(3), 525–546.

Zimmer, L. (1986). *Women guarding men*. Chicago: University of Chicago Press.

CORRECTIONAL LEADERS:
THE ADMINISTRATOR CULTURE

Previous chapters have addressed the issues of correctional leadership and organizational culture, theories of organizational culture, the relationship between organizational culture and leadership, and correctional officer culture. In this chapter, we will examine correctional administrator culture. We begin with an exploration of the dimensions of correctional administrator culture, including such topics as organizational uncertainty, policies and procedures, defining mission and vision, and leadership and conflict management. In the second section of the chapter, we examine specific focal concerns of correctional leaders, such as the relationship between correctional leadership and both politics and unions, the cultivation of leaders within the constraints of a civil service system, and correctional leadership and the public.

The final section of the chapter fleshes out the connection between leadership and organizational culture, the limitations to correctional leadership, the importance of a mission statement and vision to correctional leadership, and the significance of values to correctional leadership and organizational culture. Our purpose is to demonstrate why correctional leaders must lead and to show the connection between leadership behaviors and the formation of an organizational culture. We contend that no one is more critical to the formation of organizational culture than the correctional leader.

In essence, correctional leaders imbue within their organizations a "moral sense" (Wilson, 1989). The moral sense within a prison organization is determined, to a large degree, by the person who is in charge at the top. This is not to suggest that others in the prison hierarchy cannot be leaders or persons who instill a sense of purpose and vision in the organization. Leadership behavior can be exhibited at any level within the prison, but its most visible representation must come from that person who sits at the top of the prison hierarchy. In prison organizations, this is the warden. The warden as a correctional leader is critical to influencing organizational culture; as a correctional leader, no one is more important in shaping, influencing, and directing employees and prisoners than the warden.

With their staff, wardens direct the culture of the prison. Wardens work within an identifiable culture that is unique and different from the culture of correctional officers and middle management. An examination of the dimensions of the correctional administration culture is consistent with our suggestion in Chapter 3 that prison organizations are composed of three cultures. We begin this chapter by explicating the dimensions and elements of the correctional administrator culture.

DIMENSIONS OF CORRECTIONAL ADMINISTRATOR CULTURE

Very little research has attempted to identify the dimensions of correctional administrator culture; nevertheless, certain activities and issues dominate the correctional administrator culture. Similar to other work settings, the administrative culture of the prison reflects the concerns, routines, and activities that make up "the central tasks of human relationships within an organization" (Wilson, 1989, p. 91). For correctional administrators, this culture has a profound impact on correctional leadership in that leaders both influence and are influenced by it. The shaping of this culture, as well as the cultures of middle managers and correctional officers, is a critical activity for correctional leaders.

The dimensions of the correctional administrator culture are defined by the work setting and the tasks performed by correctional administrators. Issues faced by correctional administrators within prisons that help define their culture include: dealing with organizational uncertainty, developing policies and procedures, defining the mission, and managing conflict.

Organizational Uncertainty

"If one party needs something from another and cannot predict how that second party will behave, the second party has power over the first. In the extreme case we will do almost anything to please a madman with life-death power over us because we cannot predict which behavior will produce what reaction" (Wilson, 1989, p. 330). In the case of correctional leaders, many "madmen" direct and influence the workings of prisons. Some examples include governors, legislators, employee unions, the courts, and members of the media. Each of these entities has a potentially profound impact on the ability of correctional leaders to perform their jobs.

The unpredictable nature of the interactions with the various entities that direct and influence the prison workings produces uncertainty. The high level of uncertainty that is created by these groups is instrumental in the development of a specific organizational culture among correctional administrators. This culture is fixated on the present, and attempting to calculate how one will be affected by the actions of others is a difficult task. Moreover, the expectations of these groups are often unrealistic from the perspective of the correctional administrator, fostering an us-versus-them mentality. The product of such uncertainty is the creation of a reactive posture that is too often defensive and lacks the necessary stimulation to move prison organizations forward.

This is most evident in case studies that have examined the influence of court orders on prison systems. One of the most glaring examples of a defensive, some would even say defiant, stance to the uncertainty produced by court intervention is the case of *Ruiz v. Estelle* (1980). In this case, corrections officials in the state of Texas fought with a particularly forceful federal judge (Judge William Wayne Justice) over a 15-year period about the operations of the Texas prisons. The culture in the Texas prisons for many years was one that lacked receptivity to different ideas on how prisons should be run. The culture that had developed supported violence and brutality toward prisoners as a way of life (Martin & Ekland-Olson, 1987). Corrections officials in the state of Texas viewed the intrusion by the courts as not only unacceptable in many instances, but also an affront to the existing *culture* of their prisons and their ways of doing business.

In the administrative culture of the prison, anything that produces increased uncertainty is problematic. Within such a culture, very little can be done to change the existing status quo, and as such, correctional administrators are left with very few options to address the problems they face. The quest to make everything certain engenders a bureaucratic mentality that is antithetical to effective correctional leadership. The product of such a culture is micromanagement, that is, being overly concerned with details and existing ways of doing business. There is very little room for the development of flexibility when confronting changing and unyielding internal and external environments (Nanus, 1992).

Policies and Procedures

The search for uniform and appropriate policies to confront the multitude of issues faced by prison officials and staff is important. This dimension of the administrative culture is especially difficult for many correctional administrators to handle. On the one hand, well-written polices and procedures are essential to the functioning of prisons, yet on the other hand, policies and procedures can take on a life of their own, almost to the point of having religious significance to some correctional administrators, and serve to inhibit or discourage appropriate risk taking on the part of employees.

A correctional administrator from the California Department of Corrections who attended a workshop directed by one of the authors relayed the following story concerning the dilemma faced by correctional administrators when confronted with the everyday realities of prison life and organizational policies and procedures:

> One day we had a whole bus of late transfers from another prison who needed to have pillowcases for their pillows. We had a policy that stated no pillowcases could be given to inmates during the night. They had to be given only during the day shift. As the correctional captain on duty, I realized that this was a minor issue and gave the authorization for pillowcases to be retrieved from the storage area and given to the inmates. The next day I was reprimanded for not following proper departmental procedure. While I knew the violation was nothing serious, what I learned was that in this prison, an allegiance to policies and procedures was absolute and that if you did violate a policy or procedure, no matter how minor, you were going to have to pay. I didn't think this was right, but I have since seen other instances where policy just didn't fit and the warden and his staff were really more concerned with controlling employees rather than addressing the everyday issues of the prison.

As with organizational uncertainty, this dimension of correctional administrator culture can serve to inhibit the kind of behavior that actually can be good for prisons. While we cannot envision a correctional environment where there is a blatant disregard for policies and procedures, correctional work is porous and requires the flexibility endemic to people processing work. Cultural cues and directions that reinforce strict adherence to policies and procedures are not only ineffective but may be dangerous to maintaining the tenuous balance among staff, prisoners, and administrators. As stated by Wright (1994), effective prison leadership requires both a tight and a loose ship. This means encouraging people to take appropriate risks, developing teamwork, empowering employees to achieve shared goals, and paying sufficient attention to the details of correctional work. All this can be achieved by the development of an administrative culture within the prison which understands that the ultimate aim of policies and procedures is a more smoothly operating correctional institution.

Defining a Mission: Diverse Expectations and Limited Resources

One of the most important dimensions of the administrative culture of a prison is defining a mission. In fact, some writers, such as Nanus (1992, p. 3) view the development of a mission statement as the central purpose of leadership in all organizations. Whether or not they want to admit it, the behaviors of correctional administrators ultimately dictate a mission statement to employees. Flowery platitudes about the direction of the organization and commitment to certain core principles and values will crumble under the reality of day-to-day behaviors if employees see that the words do not comport with leaders' behavior. Maintaining, reinforcing, and supporting a correctional mission statement is critical to influencing culture within prison organizations.

Under our three cultures model, the responsibility for influencing the cultures of middle management and correctional officers rests with the leaders up and down the prison's hierarchy. In Chapter 6, we will address this issue more concretely. For now, as a dimension of the administrative culture of the prison, the central problem is how to define a mission statement within the context of diverse expectations and limited resources. The prison is expected to achieve many things. Much of the effort of correctional administrators is directed toward recognizing these differing expectations, prioritizing them, and channeling limited resources. But what exactly should the priorities be, and what are the best methods and resources available to address them? There are no easy answers.

DiIulio (1987) states that prison managers should strive for facilities that provide *order, amenity,* and *service,* all within the context of a "control model" of prison management. Under such a model, the mission and vision of the prison are fairly clear. Prisoners are to be kept in line through strict adherence to rules and regulations. The expectations of the prison are fairly modest. As long as the prison's security is sustained and prisoner disturbances are kept to a minimum, the prison is a success. Consistent with this message is the belief in prison programs and opportunities as ways in which the order of the prison is maintained. All efforts in the prison are geared toward the control and surveillance of the inmate population. Yet, as any experienced correctional administrator will tell you, the prison is expected to do many things beyond prisoner control.

Prisons are expected to do multiple things simultaneously. They are expected to make prisoners be more tractable, yet also to provide services and treatment programming so that inmates have a better chance of success when they are released from prison than they would if nothing were done with them. There is a growing concern among many in the public that prisons have slipped into a warehousing mentality, with very little effort directed toward the improvement of prisoners. Critics of the contemporary prison have noted the dire consequences of the warehousing strategy on both correctional systems and society at large (Irwin & Austin, 2000).

In addition, correctional administrators are deluged with requests from many diverse interests to do more with their prisons and prisoners. For example, not only are prisons to be austere places where something constructive can be done with prisoners, but they are expected to engage in producing goods and services for sale. This call to make prisons "factories with fences" has been part of prison history since the invention of the penitentiary. In contemporary times, the call has been more pronounced, with states venturing into the production and distribution of many products ranging from computer hardware and software to prison-made jeans. Prison industry took off in many states across the United States in the latter part of the 20th century. As part of the mission, the practice of using inmate labor to produce goods and services has ascended among prison priorities in response to legislative and public pressure to make prisons more efficient places and to defray prison costs. Correctional leaders cannot discuss their mission without including the role of prison industries.

The 21st century prison serves as a school, a place of employment, a geriatric center, a hospital, and in a host of other functional roles that in the past would not have been part of its mission. As one correctional administrator in New York commented to one of the authors, "The business of corrections reaches beyond the custody of offenders." Prisons have evolved into places with multiple expectations chasing finite resources. With these expectations come all the attendant problems that are endemic to organizations trying to do more with less. In the past, more mainstream institutions in society addressed problems such as literacy, drug dependence, and mental health problems, to mention a just few, but for some reason these expectations have now been transferred to correctional institutions.

This is no more true than in the case of the mentally ill offender. The entire criminal justice system has been overwhelmed by the influx of mentally ill offenders, and prisons have been mandated to provide treatment for them, even though treatment as part of a correctional regimen is a difficult challenge. What is problematic is both how this treatment is to be provided within correctional institutions and how it is to be subsidized.

A larger issue is what expectations of prisons in terms of correctional treatment are reasonable. What can we expect to achieve with correctional treatment in prison settings, and what types of intervention are the most effective with what types of offenders? Again, correctional administrators are often conflicted about what they can do and what is possible given that their resources are limited. More often than not, they are forced, out of necessity, to select those programs that are manageable and practical given the constraints they face. In this situation, defining a mission that is too broad or overly ambitious is not in a leader's best interests, nor is it possible.

For many correctional leaders, defining the mission is not a singular task. The mission statement of a department of corrections or a prison reflects an amalgam of interests and expressions. Defining correctional mission includes the preferences and peculiarities of many interests (i.e., correctional stakeholders) that are both internal and external to the corrections department and the prison. Paying attention to these interests is often difficult because these concerns reflect competing values and ideas on how correctional work is to be accomplished. Moreover, some correctional stakeholders are more important than others. For many correctional leaders, figuring out the important interests from the unimportant interests is a challenging task, but clearly some have more influence over the process of defining a correctional mission than others.

Most importantly, the defining of the mission must be placed within the context of limited resources. As a California correctional administrator suggested to one of the authors:

> Correctional work would be more manageable if we had more funds, but that is not a realistic expectation. We already have almost a five billion dollar budget, and you can bet all the social service people, the health care people, and the higher education people are ready to criticize us as a waste of the taxpayers' money. We are going to have to figure out a way to do what we do better and more efficiently.

This is why defining a reasonable correctional mission is so important. Later in the chapter, we will discuss the importance of a correctional *vision* to correctional leadership. For now, we point out that defining this mission is problematic and filled with conflict and disagreement among competing interests.

Leadership and Conflict Management

James Gomez, a former director of the California Department of Corrections, once stated that one of the most important tasks he performed was to manage conflict. Conflict is a necessary element of change within all organizations. Within correctional organizations such as prisons, conflict management is a central activity for correctional administrators. Since correctional administrators spend so much time attending to conflict or the fallout of conflict situations, it is a significant element defining their culture; how this conflict is managed defines a core dimension of their culture. For many correctional administrators, "putting out fires" and managing conflict is their primary activity, yet correctional managers and leaders have different views on conflict and on how it should be addressed.

For many correctional managers, conflict resolution is managed through the hierarchy and an appeal to policies and procedures. This is not to suggest that other methods of conflict resolution are not possible or desirable; in fact, a central element of good conflict management is a recognition that conflict can be handled both formally and informally. It is the *view* of conflict within correctional organizations that is critical. For traditional correctional managers, dealing with conflict means trying to eradicate it or minimize it. For correctional leaders, however, conflict is accepted as a key element or part of the correctional landscape that is actually good for the organization. What is critical to correctional leadership is how conflict is both viewed and used by leaders to enhance the prison's mission statement and purpose.

Conflict is an essential part of defining the organization's mission and direction. As a dimension of correctional culture, the management of conflict is more a statement of how correctional leaders understand and interpret their mission than anything else. Jinkins and Jinkins (1998) describe how conflict is viewed by poor leadership and good leadership:

> [W]hen people come together in an organization and attempt to allow their own cultures to inform and interpret, in fact, to form the vision of that organization and that organization's purposes and goals, there is bound to be real conflict over the identity, vision, and goals . . . of the organization grounded in conflicting understanding of what is good and true derived from members' own cultural and social backgrounds. Poor leadership attempts to homogenize these various and divergent voices into a single voice. Good leadership cultivates the discordant plurality for the sake of the good of the society. (p. 117)

We would add that effective correctional leadership cultivates the varied interests for the good of the prison. A distinctive characteristic of effective correctional leadership is how leaders interpret the differences among their employees in such a way that conflict is used to advance the mission of the organization as determined by correctional staff, various stakeholders, and relevant parties. A cultural milieu is constructed predicated on the belief that conflict serves the purpose of unifying persons toward a common mission that is of their own creation. Correctional leaders distinguish themselves from correctional managers, in part, by how well they foster an organizational climate that values conflict as a prerequisite to defining the mission. In addition, conflict serves the instrumental purpose of unifying discordant elements within an organization.

For correctional leaders, conflict is liberating; for correctional managers, conflict is enslaving. Through the conflict resolution process, the measure of a correctional leader is determined. Moreover, how correctional leaders and managers address conflict will, in part, define the "tone" of the correctional culture within the prison. Correctional administrators, either managers or leaders, who send the message to employees that differing views and opinions will not be tolerated engender a correctional culture that inhibits divergent expressions and minimizes employee investment within the organization. On the other hand, a view of conflict resolution that encourages conflict as a necessary aspect of defining the mission of the prison is painful but valuable. By recognizing the important contribution that conflict can make to prison organizations, correctional leaders empower their employees and encourage them to think of new ways to contribute to the mission of the organization they help to create.

Correctional leaders are responsible for advancing a culture that recognizes the importance of conflict in bringing diverse groups and interests together so that the mission statement is relevant to the prison's success. Too often, correctional administrators have attempted to eradicate or homogenize conflict, with the product being a stifled and inhibited group of employees who only know the existing ways of doing business. This limits employee creativity and sends the message that divergent expressions are not to be tolerated. Such a cultural setting within a prison organization is not effective and is inimical to the long-term health of the organization. How correctional leaders foster a prison culture that recognizes the importance of conflict to the success of the correctional mission is a central activity that defines their style of leadership and long-term effectiveness.

CORRECTIONAL LEADERSHIP: FOCAL CONCERNS

In addition to dealing with organizational uncertainty, developing policies and procedures, defining a mission, and managing conflict as central activities, prison administrators also have to deal with a variety of concerns that influence the prison's culture. Administrators react to many issues and situations, yet some concerns are more relevant than others, and some are significant in that they engender specific cultural norms in the prison. Focal concerns of correctional administrators include the following: correctional leadership and politics; leadership, management, and unions; cultivating leaders within the civil service system; and correctional leadership and the public.

Correctional Leadership and Politics

The topic of politics and correctional leadership is significant within corrections. Across the United States, many correctional leaders lament the role of politics in the operations of their correctional facilities. *Politics,* for many correctional leaders, is a dirty word. Often politics is dismissed as the dark side of correctional leadership. Nevertheless, any discussion of correctional leadership must consider the role of politics.

Politics means different things to different people. At one level, when correctional leaders talk about politics, they are talking about the *internal* dynamics within their organizations. At this level, politics refers to the workings and the push-and-pull of everyday life across the various departments within a prison organization. Such operational areas as budgeting, finance, personnel, and administration have their own unique political issues. Other internal political questions revolve around custody versus noncustody personnel and the appropriate use of resources. At the internal level, politics is the fodder for discussion, debate, disagreement, and concern over how the prison will realize its mission and purposes.

At another level, politics may be considered *external*. At this level, politics concerns the activities and expectations of people external to the prison, such as the legislature, the governor's office, the courts, public interest groups, and various stakeholders. This level of politics concerns itself with how external forces shape and influence the operations of the prison. Many correctional leaders consider this level of politics more problematic than internal politics, since they have less visible control over external entities.

Politics takes on a different form for correctional leaders at the external level. Dealing with politicians, citizens' groups, and the courts has been a challenging and daunting task for correctional leaders. In Chapter 1, we discussed how the challenges of the external environment, particularly from the courts, have been difficult for correctional administrators. This is the level of politics at which correctional leaders have fallen short of the mark. During the latter part of the 20th century, correctional leaders acted more like managers than leaders in addressing the problems and issues they faced from the external world. Many correctional leaders have not made an understanding of the political process a part of their agenda, even though external politics plays such an important part in what they do and ultimately affects how they are viewed as correctional leaders (Breed, 1998).

One example of where correctional leaders have missed the mark in politics is in their relationships with governors and key legislative personnel. One author of this text has spent seven years working with a department of corrections to improve its leadership education program. In that program, discussions of events and situations involving the governor of the state and the department of corrections were often reduced to "well, that's politics." The outcomes of these interactions were perceived by many program participants to be adverse to the department of corrections. The fatalism of their views made the author inquire into how their situation with the governor's office could be improved. To the author's surprise, many of the correctional leaders knew very little about the political process, nor were they aware of how their own legislative liaison office worked with the legislature and the governor's office on pending legislation affecting the department of corrections. Moreover, many of the correctional administrators knew only to *accept* the status quo as it related to the governor's office and had no idea about, nor any interest in, challenging the process and questioning how the status quo could be changed. In fact, many of the participants formed their understanding of the relationship with the governor's office on rumor and hearsay. Many could not support their limited understanding with any evidence beyond anecdotes of failure by those brave few who tried to change the system and were ultimately relegated to some undesirable post with the department while awaiting their proverbial "golden handshake" of retirement.

Being good managers, these correctional leaders reacted to whatever was imposed upon them. Very few thought *leadership* was actually possible or desirable. When the author asked them what alternative arrangement could be devised to improve their situations, most participants were at a loss for words. When the author provided some key distinguishing characteristics of managers and leaders and asked the participants to identify leaders within their department, they had difficulty coming up with any names. In fact, some even suggested that external politics were so influential within the department of corrections, there really was no genuine interest in cultivating leaders, and that the department created the leadership development program simply as a symbolic gesture to the legislature and the governor's office to demonstrate a commitment to changing their culture and existing ways of doing business when, in reality, the program was merely a triumph of style over substance.

Primary questions remain. What is the proper role of correctional leadership when it comes to external politics? Are correctional leaders only billiard balls to be knocked around by the vagaries of external groups, such as the governor's office or the legislature? Is leadership a passive endeavor for correctional leaders? What can be reasonably accomplished by correctional leaders given the influence and perceived power of certain external groups on prisons? Addressing these questions and others is important to the success of correctional leaders. As a focal concern, no other issue has more relevance to the future of correctional leadership than politics. How correctional leaders respond to both their internal and external political environments is a measure of how successful they will be. Chapters 6 and 7 will be devoted to answering the questions asked here; but for now, it is important to comprehend the relevance of politics to effective correctional leadership and how it influences the administrative culture of the prison.

Leadership, Management, and the Unions

As a focal concern, the issue of correctional unions is becoming more pressing, particularly with the growth and proliferation of both public and private correctional facilities. Across the country, correctional employees are growing in number, and their power is slowly rising within the political arena. Most correctional unions tend to be small and to exert minimal political influence. In some areas of the United States, however, correctional unions are very powerful. In California, for example, the California Correctional Peace Officers Association (CCPOA) is a significant political actor and has aggressively lobbied with the state legislature and the governor's office for its members' interests. In fact, in gubernatorial elections in California, the CCPOA was one of the top financial contributors toward the election of former Governor Pete Wilson and current Governor Gray Davis. For correctional leaders, this type of political clout has been unsettling and difficult to address.

In California, the CCPOA has been so successful in lobbying with political figures that often correctional leaders perceive themselves to be held hostage by the union. While the CCPOA has taken a proactive posture within the political arena, very little has been done by leaders within the California Department of Corrections to advance their interests and to work with the union to bring about conditions that are conducive to both groups. In fact, the historical relationship between the CCPOA and correctional leaders within the California Department of Corrections has been strained, to say the least. Many correctional leaders in California view the CCPOA as the enemy, an entity to be viewed with suspicion and distrust, even though the ascendency of the CCPOA, both politically and organizationally, can be traced to the draconian leadership and management practices of the past.

Such a view of correctional unions is not unique to California. One popular text on correctional management devotes an entire chapter to correctional unions, entitling it "Unions: Avoiding Them When Possible and Living with Them When Necessary" (Phillips & McConnell, 1996). Implicit and explicit messages are replete within the chapter to suggest that unions are an unavoidable part of correctional management and that they are, in some cases, a bad thing. The authors even go so far as to offer a strategy and a series of steps to prevent the creation of correctional unions, while recognizing that often union organizing is a direct reaction to the practices and failures of correctional administration. Such a view and strategy of dealing with correctional unions is counterproductive toward the development of effective correctional leadership.

Correctional unions are not the problem. Our reaction to them is the problem. As stated earlier, correctional unions are reactions to the practices of the past. The CCPOA was not created overnight; it was created in response to long-term abuses and practices that minimized correctional employees and treated them poorly. Unions reflect the fundamental differences and philosophies between managers and leaders. It is no fluke that the chapter by Phillips and McConnell (1996) mentioned earlier was written for a book on correctional management. Too many correctional managers view unions as a threat. For correctional leaders, however, unions are not a threat but an opportunity to work together in a productive fashion toward the accomplishment of the prison's mission statement. Good correctional leaders and managers understand this and exhibit leadership behaviors in dealing with their unions.

For the correctional leader, the primary concern with unions is how they should be included in the process of formulating and implementing the prison's mission statement. The union should play an influential role in the development of the prison's mission statement. The union members are the correctional rank-and-file employees who breathe life into the prison's mission statement. By viewing correctional unions as part of the process, correctional leaders provide a venue for all legitimate concerns to be voiced and heard within the prison. Instead of battling with unions, leaders should bring them on board as allies. In the end, prison culture reflects an amalgam of relationships among persons. The correctional leader is responsible for solidifying these relationships in such a way that the mission and purpose are possible. This is a tall order, and particularly problematic in correctional departments where the response to unions has been dominated by narrowly defined management strategies without regard to their impact on prison culture. Correctional leadership needs to be more vigilant and inclusive of the views of unions in the creation and implementation of the prison's mission statement and vision for the future.

Cultivating Leaders Within the Civil Service System

The public commonly complains that the central problem with public agencies, such as corrections, is that they are hamstrung by the rules and regulations of a civil service bureaucracy. Many state and federal reforms have been created to address the assumed problems with the civil service system (Rainey, 1997). Both presidents and governors have attempted to remedy the problems associated with the civil service system by increasing the degree of political oversight over public agencies, and nowhere is this more true than in the corrections field.

Many critics of corrections have argued that the increased politicization of both crime and the criminal justice system's response to crime, along with the removal of civil service protections for public employees, has made things worse for those working in corrections. These critics raise two specific concerns. First, the reforms focused on changing the civil service system have not only sought to reduce the power and influence of career civil servants, but also have placed executives and legislators in the forefront of dealing with crime. In short, crime policy has become more politicized. The increased federalization of drug laws, for example, has politicized the drug problem and devastated entire communities, particularly disadvantaged communities where, in some instances, a substantial proportion of minority men are under the control of the criminal justice system (Tonry, 1995). Additionally, the direct impact on correctional systems has been profound, most visibly on the size of correctional populations. The most direct consequences of the increased politicalization of crime have been prison overcrowding and increased public expenditures for correctional programs. This has produced an enormous number of intractable problems for correctional administrators, problems for which there are a dearth of solutions. Prison crowding is just one example; but other issues, such as the incarceration of the mentally ill, the geriatric needs of an aging prison population, and the health needs of prisoners will continue to challenge correctional leaders well into the future.

Second, critics have noted that the degree to which governors and legislators have politicized crime issues has made it is difficult for criminal justice administrators to manage and lead their organizations. Within the realm of institutional corrections, this means the degree to which the executive and legislative branches of government have attempted to micromanage prisons. In this sense, the degree of politicalization of correctional efforts makes it difficult for corrections professionals to function. Moreover, the consequences for correctional leadership are profound. The question becomes, how do you lead when many of your decisions are being reviewed (in some cases controlled) and diluted by those in political power? Is it possible to lead under such conditions? For practical correctional leaders and managers, these questions are difficult to answer.

The consequences of civil service reform and the overpoliticalization of corrections have been twofold. First, it has been difficult for correctional leaders to voice opinions that are counter to the political views of their bosses, usually governors and powerful legislators, even when they know those views are not only wrong but also harmful to correctional staff and prisoners. One of the authors of this text observed an example of this when one state department of corrections was directed by the governor's office and the state legislature to implement a "give-back" program, whereby over a period of time many prison amenities, such as weights and smoking privileges, would be taken away from prisoners. Even though correctional officials viewed such amenities as part of an incentive program for getting prisoners to behave, none of these officials would voice their concerns about the give-back program to the legislature and the governor's office. As one correctional administrator remarked to the author, "What the governor wants, the governor gets." When the author asked about the effects of such an initiative on the prison population, this correctional administrator stated that it was hard to predict the immediate impact of the program but, in his words, "The governor's give-back program sure makes my job more difficult." When the author suggested that this view was *reactive* rather than *proactive* in its approach, this correctional administrator cynically stated, "Welcome to the world of corrections."

The second consequence of civil service reform and the increased political-ization of corrections has been reduced morale among correctional staff, partic-ularly administrative personnel. A sense of fear and malaise has set in on many corrections departments, such that challenging the status quo, both within the department and external to the department, becomes difficult and problematic. Many correctional administrators are directed by their fear, and the fear is relat-ed to the degree to which they are expected to conform to the political interests of those in power.

It is difficult to lead and move an organization forward through fear. In some cases, people who have been critical of or in disagreement with a governor's policies toward corrections have been relieved of their duties or reassigned to lower positions within departments of corrections. Due to the structure of the civil service system, many employees are not protected and can be dismissed at any time. In addition, the degree to which political partisanship has influenced the hierarchy of departments of corrections has been significant. In some cases, few administrative positions within the central office of a department of correc-tions are "protected," and the entire process of warden selection may involve leg-islative oversight and governor approval. This creates a situation whereby opposing operational viewpoints concerning a state's prisons are virtually non-existent, even though many of these viewpoints are necessary for responding effectively to the challenges faced by departments of corrections. Under such arrangements, how is one to lead?

We will provide specific recommendations on how correctional leaders can respond to this situation in subsequent chapters. What is important for now is that correctional leadership is possible within a civil service system structure. Correctional leadership is sustainable within the parameters of a civil service sys-tem, however, only through a leadership development program cultivated by departments of corrections. Very few correctional departments have invested the resources, time, and energy to work toward the cultivation of leaders who can address simultaneously the problems posed by civil service reforms and the politicalization issue in corrections. As a primary focal concern for correctional leaders, how they help shape and structure their civil service systems will be crit-ical to their success. In this way, they will be providing direction on how the civil service system can be implemented to address the concerns of critics who view such a system as inefficient and regard political control as the only reasonable response to it.

Correctional Leadership and the Public

One of the more difficult things for correctional administrators to comprehend is how they are viewed by the public. For many correctional leaders, the public is an amorphous entity, almost monolithic in its form. This monolithic public, in addition, is almost always viewed as negative. The basis for this view is often incorrect. Correctional managers and leaders commonly describe the public's view of corrections as being limited and shortsighted and never in tune with the realities of correctional work. Yet, a view of the public as being monolithic is actually counterproductive on a number of grounds.

To begin, there is no monolithic public perception of corrections. There is really no public in the environment; instead, there are many *publics* that represent diverse interests and concerns (Rainey, 1997). Correctional leaders' view of the public as monolithic precludes them from seeing the differences among the many publics and, most importantly, limits their strategic decision making when addressing specific concerns. For example, prison leaders and managers talk about how "the" public views prisons negatively. When you ask these prison leaders and managers how they know this, they are often left speechless. For many of these officials, their *perceptions* of how the public views prisons are limited and misinformed. In actuality, too many prison officials really do not know what the public perceives about prisons. Moreover, not only is there a limited understanding among prison officials about the public's perception of prisons, but there is also a misguided belief that a singular response will positively alter the public's perception of prisons. Nothing could be further from the truth.

For correctional leadership to have an impact on public perception, a detailed and specific plan must be developed to address highly particularized interests found among specific actors in the public. For example, if the perception is that the legislature holds a negative and critical view of the state's prison system, then correctional leaders, to be effective, must address specific concerns that fuel that perception. If a certain legislator controls power that may affect corrections, then a specific strategy to deal with that legislator is required. Similarly, if there are specific issues of interest to particular groups in the community concerning correctional matters, then shaping and influencing their perceptions requires a highly focused action plan. Paying attention to this type of detail influences public perception. Such a strategy allows correctional leaders to demonstrate, in part, to certain publics what they are doing to address specific concerns.

Some publics are more important and relevant to corrections than others. Given the plurality of publics that correctional leaders have to address, how do they prioritize the competing and conflicting interests of the public? For effective correctional leadership, the identification of key stakeholders is crucial. Correctional leaders must concentrate on influencing those significant publics that shape the image and perceptions of corrections. So, who are these people?

For differing departments of corrections, there are different stakeholders who shape and influence public perception. Common examples of stakeholders include the following: key legislators, the governor, the media, certain private interest groups, other public entities, the courts, and other agencies in the criminal justice system. As part of the larger "public," these organizations have, in most states, a significant amount of influence over corrections. It would behoove correctional leaders to prioritize these organizations on the degree of influence they have over corrections. In one state, for example, the federal courts may have a significant role on how the public perceives corrections, as was the case in the earlier example of the relationship between one particular judge, Judge William Wayne Justice, and the Texas Department of Corrections. Scholarship documented the vitriolic relationship that existed between that judge and the Texas Department of Corrections throughout the 1980s (Crouch & Marquart, 1989; Martin & Ekland-Olson, 1987).

By conceptualizing the public as being composed of multiple publics with varying and diverse interests and disparate levels of power and influence, correctional leaders can deal more effectively with public perceptions concerning corrections. Only through such an analytical approach does the term *public* have any meaning for correctional leaders. Without such a strategy, correctional leaders are left with a plethora of perceptions concerning their image that are often inaccurate and counterproductive. In the long run, the lack of a proactive plan to address the public creates more confusion and resorts in haphazard attempts to understand and correctly perceive what the public wants and demands of corrections. Such an approach is antithetical to effective leadership. Correctional leaders must identify their key stakeholders, distinguish those who are influential from those who are not, and develop a strategy to inform and influence these stakeholders and to enlist them in their mission statement and vision for corrections. In short, correctional leaders must lead, not simply manage and react. Nowhere is this more important than in their development of an administrative culture consistent with the aims and values of the larger organizational culture.

CORRECTIONAL ADMINISTRATOR CULTURE AND ORGANIZATIONAL CULTURE

Leadership and Organizational Culture: Why Should Leaders Lead?

In an important book entitled *On Becoming a Leader,* the noted organizational theorist Warren Bennis (1989) argues that effective leaders "master the context" rather than surrender to it. Bennis is referring to the outlook and direction that leadership provides to an organization. Similarly, Nanus (1992, pp. 11–12) suggests that in order to be effective in today's world, leaders have to balance four delicate processes: the use of relationship skills with workers and managers; understanding the importance of the external environment to one's success; shaping and influencing all aspects of the organization; and comprehending and anticipating the future. All these processes are critical to successful correctional leadership, and the theme that ties all four of them together is organizational culture.

Nothing is more important to correctional leadership than the creation of an organizational culture. Creating this organizational culture requires all four processes listed by Nanus and more. For correctional leaders, the creation of an organizational culture means comprehending corrections as people work. The backbone of this work is predicated on relationships among all those who function in the prison—managers, officers, support staff, and prisoners. In addition, this organizational culture is influenced by the external world, as noted in the discussion on correctional leadership and the public. This organizational culture influences all processes within the prison, and it must be based on anticipation and planning for the future.

Correctional leaders should lead because it is incumbent on them to make sure these processes and issues are attended to by managers and other correctional staff. Correctional leadership defines the parameters within which employees function in the prison. All the functional aspects of the prison, however, are filtered through the prism of organizational culture. The correctional leader is the one who works with others in defining and structuring this prism and assisting correctional employees in formulating organizational values and the mission statement of the prison. This is why correctional leadership is so important. Through a recognition of the aforementioned processes, correctional leaders define organizational culture. They set the tone, or what we referred to in the beginning of the chapter as the "moral sense," of the organization, as well as determining how the prison will function. Through their leadership and attention to these issues, organizational culture becomes visible and relevant to all those who work in the prison. Assumptions about the *correct* ways to do things become routine and accepted and are part of the organization's vocabulary and actions; attending to these assumptions and the processes that define organizational culture is the leader's responsibilities. Once these assumptions and attendant practices are accepted and recognized by those who work in the organization, possible advancement and change are more likely (Schein, 1997).

Limitations to Correctional Leadership

Although the creation of organizational culture is extremely important to correctional leadership, being an effective correctional leader is not a *panacea*. Correctional leadership involves paying attention to many issues. Many things affect correctional administration, only some of which can be reasonably controlled and influenced. For example, the state of the economy has both direct and indirect effects on the operations of corrections, but there is little that correctional leaders can do to manipulate the economy. Correctional leaders have to work in the confines of what is possible; some things are just beyond their control. This is not to suggest, however, that fatalism and pessimism should reign supreme. Knowing what is possible and impossible in corrections is what, in part, defines effective correctional leadership.

Correctional leaders must attempt to distinguish their vision from fantasy. While utopia is appealing to many, correctional leaders do not have the luxury of thinking in a utopian manner. Too many pressures obviate such thinking. For correctional leaders, the process of realizing their vision lies in two things: the mission statement and a statement of values. What correctional leaders can accomplish rests within an understanding of their purpose and the values they seek to promulgate among correctional employees. This is why a mission statement and a statement of values are so critical to effective correctional leadership. They allow correctional leaders to distinguish reality from fantasy, what is possible from what is impossible, and most importantly, they provide the platform by which both internal and external constituencies can understand the purposes and direction of the prison.

Correctional leadership, then, has a firm ground in what is possible, even though what is possible must have some hope and vision for the correctional future. It is apparent that the world of corrections is changing rapidly and that for correctional leaders to respond effectively to this world, they are going to need a mission statement, some core values, and a vision that can respond to these changes. By incorporating these elements into a strategic plan, leaders begin to produce successful organizational and cultural change. This involves both the transformation and transmission of correctional culture, the focus of the next chapter in this book. We conclude this chapter by examining why a correctional vision and values are so critical to effective correctional leadership, and why sending the right message is so important to influencing the three cultures within prison organizations.

The Importance of a Correctional Vision and Mission Statement

Leadership consultants James Kouzes and Barry Posner (1997) suggest in their book, *The Leadership Challenge: How to Keep Getting Extraordinary Things Done in Organizations,* that a mission statement and vision are important to organizations. A vision is where the organization wants to be and encompasses a conceptualization of the future. This future state is uplifting and positive in focus. More importantly, this future state is engendered out of the current dissatisfaction with how things are accomplished in the organization. In effect, a vision seeks to redirect where an organization is going. Kouzes and Posner (1997) state:

> Discovering a vision for your organization is similar in many ways to the initial stages of preparing for an expedition. You feel a strong inner sense of dissatisfaction with the way things are in your . . . organization and have an equally strong belief that things don't have to be this way. Envisioning the future begins with a vague desire to do something that would challenge yourself and others. (p. 96)

For prisons, it would be fair to state that many leaders, managers, and officers feel this sense of dissatisfaction. The importance of a vision lies in its potential to offer hope and an agenda for doing things differently within the prison. Many correctional employees are waiting for someone to help create a new vision for their prison. In short, they are waiting for someone to lead.

The mission statement and vision serve the purpose of collectively defining the goals of the prison and where it wants to be. During a leadership training session, one correctional administrator relayed to one of the authors how a malaise had set in at his prison and the frustration he was feeling because current operations were counterproductive. The author asked whether there was a mission statement for the prison and a vision of where the prison was headed. The administrator responded, "There is a reason why the officers call the warden 'Mushroom George.' Mushrooms like to be kept in the dark." In this example, not only was there no mission statement or vision, but there was virtually no leadership or management in the prison. Correctional employees of the prison had fallen into a rut of organizational indifference and apathy. In fact, months later the prison hit the national news wire because of the brutality some correctional officers had visited upon inmates and the staging of "gladiator games" among rival inmate gang leaders.

For a correctional mission and vision to have meaning, the initial creation of the statement must lie with leaders. As a process of determining what values and vision the prison wants, the various stakeholders, both internal and external to the prison, must be identified. The vision of the prison becomes an expression of where these stakeholders want the prison to be in the future. Moreover, by developing a mission and vision statement, correctional leaders provide the essential impetus for all persons in the prison to have vested interest in the prison's future. We will explicate this point further in Chapter 6, but for now, the mission statement and vision of the prison not only serve as hope for the future, but also assist correctional leaders in fostering a specific organizational culture, a culture predicated on the values of relevant stakeholders in the prison operations. The questions become: What are the appropriate values for a prison to espouse? Why are correctional leaders' values so important in influencing correctional culture?

Correctional Leadership: What Are the Values of the Leader?

Scholarship and academic debates concerning the purposes of prisons have raged for decades. Some contemporary writers see the prison as a place where punishment is expected, but say this punishment should be placed within the context of what a civilized society demands of its prisons (Johnson, 1996). Others are precise in what they expect prisons to accomplish (DiIulio, 1987, p. 50). Yet, what is left out of the discussion is what values undergird correctional practices.

Discussions with numerous correctional administrators over the years have convinced us that, for many of them, the core values that define a prison are safety and security. All prison activities center around the maintenance of safety and security for everyone in the prison, including staff, inmates, and others. As umbrella terms, the values of safety and security structure the parameters of the mission statement and vision for the prison. All other values emanate from the central concern that prison leaders, managers, and staff have about the safety and security of everyone in the prison. As core values, they define what is possible and what is not possible for the prison. Safety and security concerns are central among the values of correctional personnel in any correctional mission statement or vision.

Among correctional leaders, personal values they want to transmit to correctional employees must be placed within the context of these two larger organizational values. Such values determine the mission statement and vision of the prison in a way that both preserves the correctional past as well as defines what is likely in the future. Correctional leaders must not lose sight of the past, yet they cannot be constrained by it either. The prison's past surely serves as a prologue for the future. Individual correctional leader values must be placed within the context of the prison's values. Our experience has been that no individual values of correctional leaders will ever have the influence needed to affect organizational culture unless there is a tacit recognition of the importance of safety and security within prisons. Leaders, therefore, must be aware of how their values either support or are in opposition to these core organizational values. Nanus (1992) notes the importance of individual leader values and organizational values when trying to affect organizational culture:

> Leaders must always understand their own values, as well as the values and culture prevailing in their organizations, because these values determine whether a new sense of direction will be enthusiastically embraced, reluctantly accepted, or rejected as inappropriate. (p. 52)

This discussion of correctional values does not mean that other values are not important to the prison or that internal and external stakeholders do not expect the correctional vision to incorporate other values. Rehabilitative and treatment concerns, for example, are values that prisons have espoused in the past. Even though this past may be checkered and uneven in its expression of treatment values, this does not decrease the legitimacy of these values among many correctional professionals and persons in general society. In fact, research has demonstrated that the public recognizes the importance of rehabilitation programming for prisoners. The scholar Francis Cullen, among others, has documented the importance of rehabilitation programming to prisons and, more importantly, the expectation of the public that prisons will make genuine efforts to implement such programs for prisoners (Cullen et al., 1993).

Thus far the discussion has focused on organizational values, but what about the personal values of correctional leaders? What values do we want to see expressed by correctional leaders? There is no easy answer. Research on leadership has focused on the importance to organizations of such values as honesty, competence, the ability to look forward, and supportive relationships. All these values may be important within the correctional context, yet for values to have meaning within prisons, there must be some type of consensus among stakeholders about what the core values of the prison will be.

In a leadership training session held by one of the authors, correctional administrators were asked what five values would be most important for correctional administrators to hold. In rank order, the following were noted by administrators: honesty, competence, trustworthiness, fair-mindedness, and open-mindedness. When the correctional administrators were asked to suggest the five organizational values they would like to see promulgated by the prison, they mentioned the following: security, safety, societal protection, concern for people including prisoners, and cost efficiency. When the author asked these same administrators how individual values may conflict with organizational values, they had difficulty in responding. When the point was pursued further with an example of how being fair to prisoners could mean holding correctional personnel more accountable for their practices and behaviors in the prison, very few administrators agreed with this view. Instead, for many of these administrators, fairness meant being fair only with correctional employees, not with prisoners. When the author noted the unevenness of such a view, especially when the administrators had stated earlier that concern and fairness should be for all in the prison, there was silence in the room. When asked about the origin of this distinction between prisoners and staff on the dimension of fairness, one administrator stated that the difference between staff and prisoners was part of the *tradition* and *culture* of the prison.

The assumptions about prisoners and correctional staff are an integral part of the culture of the prison and reflect entrenched values. For effective correctional leadership to exist, a proper identification of the consistencies and inconsistencies in personal and organizational values must occur. Such an exercise serves as a point of departure for correctional leaders to arrive at a consensus among the various internal and external stakeholders on what the values of the prison will be. Much of correctional leadership effort should be directed toward arriving at this consensus among significant actors.

Sending the Message: What Correctional Leadership Is All About

The remaining two chapters of the book will address how correctional leaders can transform and transmit correctional culture to be effective leaders in the 21st century. The purpose of these chapters will be to demonstrate that leadership behaviors are critical for prisons. Effective correctional leadership works toward the development of a mission statement and a vision. The mission statement and vision of the prison must be defined by those relevant members of the prison's internal and external environment, and a clearly articulated and consistent set of values must be engendered by correctional leaders and sustained through continuous efforts. A commitment to the prison's mission statement and vision will hinge on the involvement of all correctional staff directed fundamentally toward maintaining a secure and safe place where prisoner improvement is possible.

This correctional message can be sent only after correctional leaders commit themselves to addressing issues of organizational culture. The moral sense of a prison is determined by the efforts of correctional leaders. How well correctional leaders are able to transform and transmit organizational culture within the prison is the true benchmark of their success as leaders. The transformation and transmission of correctional culture is predicated on the belief that current operations are either insufficient or unable to meet the demands of internal and external stakeholders. We turn our attention in the next chapter to correctional culture transformation and transmission.

CASE SCENARIO   *Who Provides Correctional Treatment?*

Warden Thomas Carey was a veteran of the department of corrections. He had risen from the rank of correctional officer to the highest position within the prison, all in a short period of 10 years. He was one of the "new" types of prison wardens: educated, articulate, and with a yearning to do things in the prison that his predecessors would never have considered. At the forefront of his ideas was to improve the quantity and quality of correctional services in the

(continued)

Case Scenario continued

prison and beyond. He was particularly interested in having the treatment staff interact and work more positively with the custodial staff, but his vision for the prison was more than that.

Warden Carey envisioned a time in the near future when there would be more integration of treatment services among the various providers both in and out of the prison. Current prison operations were haphazard and lacked a clear focus and discernable outcomes. Moreover, once the prisoner left the institution, there was no continuation of services beyond the prison. The relationship with the parole division was vitriolic at best and contentious at worst. Warden Carey's vision was to enable a prisoner to begin treatment services while incarcerated and continue those same services when released on parole. In this way, prisoners would have a fighting chance of reducing their risk of returning to prison.

Although Warden Carey's vision was uplifting and inspiring to many, both at headquarters and in the prison, the most staunch critics were in his own backyard. Many of his own employees viewed the idea as "pie in the sky." Carey had expected his most vociferous critics to be the custodial staff, particularly those in the old guard who viewed any changes as more work for them with limited benefits. What he found, however, was that the treatment staff was most opposed to his vision. Much of their concern centered around what they perceived as a diminution of their prestige and authority in the department. Under Warden Carey's vision of integrated treatment services, final results, either successes or failures, would be owned by treatment staff in the parole division, not the prison division.

For these prison treatment personnel, this meant a potential loss of funding. In addition, many of these personnel viewed themselves as the primary providers of supportive services for prisoners. Inmates were more closely monitored within the prison, and greater supervision of them was possible. Once prisoners were on the street, the parole division could not provide the same level of individual service, and when offenders failed, the prison could be unjustly blamed. Under current arrangements, the treatment units within the prisons controlled a vast majority of the resources devoted toward the rehabilitation of prisoners. Under Warden Carey's new program, this would drastically change.

What Warden Carey saw as his most formidable challenge was the alteration of the *cultural* expectations of prison treatment staff that they would be the primary providers of services to inmates in the department and that the parole division would have a minimal say in the matter. Warden Carey summed up the difficulties he faced in changing these cultural expectations when he asked the following question at a staff meeting: "Does anyone in here believe the parole division is part of the department of corrections?" No one answered.

Case Scenario Questions

1. Is Warden Carey's vision realistic? What do you believe are the significant obstacles he faces in changing the cultural expectations of the treatment staff in the prison?

2. Who are the stakeholders, both internal and external, who might have a vested interest in Warden Carey's vision for integrated treatment services? Are some of these stakeholders more relevant than other stakeholders? If there are some significant stakeholders, what will Warden Carey need to do to get them to agree with this vision?

3. What specific values are present in Warden Carey's vision for integrated treatment services? What are the values of the treatment personnel in the prison? How are the values of Warden Carey's vision different from the values of the treatment staff in the prison? Can competing values be reconciled in this scenario? Is so, how? If not, why not?

REFERENCES

Bennis, W. (1989). *On becoming a leader.* Reading, MA: Addision-Wesley.

Breed, A. F. (1998). Corrections: A victim of situational ethics. *Crime and Delinquency, 44*(1), 9–18.

Crouch, B., & Marquart, J. (1989). *An appeal to justice: Litigated reform of Texas prisons.* Austin, TX: University of Texas Press.

Cullen, F., Latessa, E., Burton, V., & Lombardo, L. (1993, February). The correctional orientation of prison wardens: Is the rehabilitative ideal supported? *Criminology, 31,* 69–92.

DiIulio, J. (1987). *Governing prisons: A comparative study of correctional management.* New York: Free Press.

Irwin, J., & Austin, J. (2000). *It's about time: America's imprisonment binge* (3rd ed.). Belmont, CA: West/Wadsworth.

Jinkins, M., & Jinkins, D. B. (1998). *The character of leadership: Political realism and public virtue in nonprofit organizations.* San Francisco: Jossey-Bass.

Johnson, R. (1996). *Hard time: Understanding and reforming the prison* (2nd ed.). Belmont, CA: Wadsworth.

Kouzes, J., & Posner, B. (1997). *The leadership challenge: How to keep getting extraordinary things done in organizations.* San Francisco: Jossey-Bass.

Martin, S., & Ekland-Olson, S. (1987). *Texas prisons: The walls came tumbling down.* Austin, TX: Texas Monthly Press.

Nanus, B. (1992). *Visionary leadership.* San Francisco: Jossey-Bass.

Phillips, R., & McConnell, C. (1996). *The effective corrections manager: Maximizing staff performance in demanding times.* Gaithersburg, MD: Aspen.

Rainey, H. (1997). *Understanding and managing public organizations* (2nd ed.). San Francisco: Jossey-Bass.

Ruiz v. Estelle. (1980). 503 F. Supp. 1265, 1277–1279 (S.D. Texas).

Schein, E. (1997). *Organizational culture and leadership* (2nd ed.). San Francisco: Jossey-Bass.

Tonry, M. (1995). *Malign neglect: Race, crime, and punishment in America.* New York: Oxford University Press.

Wilson, J. (1989). *Bureaucracy: What government agencies do and why they do it.* New York: Basic Books.

Wright, K. (1994). *Effective prison leadership.* Binghamton, NY: William Neil.

CREATING, TRANSMITTING, AND TRANSFORMING CORRECTIONAL CULTURE

In the previous chapter, we discussed the importance of mission, vision, and values to correctional culture. In this chapter, we will discuss the creation, transmission, and transformation processes necessary to develop a correctional culture. Earlier we described the concept of "three cultures" found within prisons: administrators, middle managers, and correctional officers. We use this model as a heuristic device to provide a framework upon which to build an understanding of how correctional culture can be influenced and shaped by correctional leaders.

The three-cultures model is not an exhaustive or definitive representation of correctional culture. The prison contains other groups that influence correctional culture, for example, medical personnel and treatment staff. The "three-cultures" model, however, provides a useful way for correctional leaders to comprehend the intricacies of their institutions while recognizing that they are the central actors in the creation, transmission, and transformation of their correctional culture. Only by achieving such understanding can leaders effectively respond to the challenges the prison faces as well as the expectations and demands of the relevant parties in the external environment.

HOW CORRECTIONAL LEADERS CREATE CORRECTIONAL CULTURE

Schein (1997, p. 211) suggests that organizational culture emanates from three sources. First, the beliefs, values, and assumptions of founders of the organization are critical to defining and creating organizational culture. The correctional literature clearly documents the role that founding leaders of prison systems have played on the cultures of their prisons. Some of the correctional leaders of the past (e.g., George Beto in Texas, Joseph Ragen in Illinois, and Richard McGee in California) had a profound influence on the creation of specific cultural beliefs about prisons and prisoners in their respective systems. Earlier we examined the legacy these individuals left not only on their respective prison systems, but also on the history of American corrections.

What defined individuals such as Beto, Ragen, and McGee as "founders" was the point at which they took over their prison systems. In the cases of McGee in California and Beto in Texas, they were placed in charge of correctional systems at points in time when their states were making changes to modernize the prison systems. McGee, for example, was the first director of the California Department of Corrections in 1944 and had a significant impact on the culture and operations of the prison system for decades to come (Glaser, 1995). Similarly, Beto ran the Texas Department of Corrections from 1962 to 1972 and was declared the chief architect of a management model that made the Texas prisons the safest in the country (DiIulio, 1987). Although not a director of corrections in the state of Illinois, Ragen was warden at Stateville penitentiary for over 30 years and was considered a significant person in the creation of a particular strategy for leading and managing prisons. In short, these correctional leaders of the past were not only "founders" within the context of the organizations they led, but they were also creators of culture. These leaders left each prison system with a lasting impression of how prisons should be led and managed, but most importantly, they created specific *cultural* assumptions, beliefs, attitudes, and artifacts that had a profound impact on the operations of their prisons for generations to come.

A second source of culture within organizations is the learning experiences of group members as their organization evolves (Schein, 1997, p. 211). Organizations are constantly changing and evolving to adapt to the influences they face. Within prisons, there are a multitude of influences. The interactions between staff and inmates, for example, are numerous and changing, even though patterns of interactions become routinized. How correctional officers understand their roles becomes contingent, to a large degree, on these patterned interactions with inmates and the cultural notions that evolve about appropriate strategies and mechanisms to control and affect the inmate population. Soon an understanding is reached and accepted among members on how to behave and interact in the prison. Much of the prisoner socialization literature, the recent correctional officer research, and the nascent correctional administrator accounts reflect how persons interact and affect one another from differing cultural norms found within the prison setting (Farkas & Manning, 1997).

A final source of organizational culture are the beliefs, values, and assumptions brought into the organization by new members and leaders (Schein, 1997, p. 211). It is here that the problematic nature of leadership becomes apparent for prison leaders. For decades, in both practice and understanding, prisons were closed organizations, with very little permeability from external forces. In fact, traditional ideas on prison management expressed the exclusivity and uniqueness of the prison by treating it as a monolithic entity that could be managed and led by adherence to classically oriented principles of chain-of-command, strict hierarchy, and rigid rules and regulations (Houston, 1999). In modern times, however, adherence to these principles has become a source of conflict in prison organizations that have been inundated by external groups demanding changes in how prisons are run.

Jacobs's (1977) analysis of Stateville penitentiary highlighted how prisons were transformed from closed organizations to more open ones. For the most part, prisons were at the periphery of society until the early 1960s, when the massive social and political changes occurring in the United States influenced their operations. The prison then became part of "mass society," with all the attendant problems that this shift in location produced. No longer could prisons be viewed as closed systems; now they were considered to be malleable organizations, with their boundaries being accessible and open to all the contingencies that accessibility engenders. For prisons, this meant not only new types of prisoners, but also new types of employees, managers, and leaders. These new persons in the prison demanded new things from prison leadership. Some prisoners, for example, became politicized, while others sought more tangible items from prison leadership. For some researchers, such a shift and change in prisoners, correctional staff, and prisons created conditions where turmoil was common (Irwin, 1980).

As the prison became more open, correctional staff (including correctional officers), management personnel, and other workers understood their roles as fundamentally different from those of their predecessors. They demanded changes in how the prison was run. Correctional officers, for example, saw the influence the courts had in advancing inmates' rights and felt that a retreat to the walls was an appropriate response (Jacobs, 1977). They became defensive and concerned about the purpose and direction of the prison. Correctional officers in some states met these legal challenges through unionization and increased political awareness. In the previous chapter, we discussed how powerful the California Correctional Peace Officers' Union has become in that state. Much of its current success can be traced to the changes that occurred in the California Department of Corrections during the 1960s, 1970s, and 1980s and correctional officers' perceived loss of authority and control over prisoners.

Moreover, along with the increasing number of legal challenges and the influence of powerful groups in the external environment of the prison, other parties began to have an impact on correctional culture in a way that left traditional prison management striving for new coping strategies. Changes in legislation and court action concerning the delivery of medical services to prisoners, the increased proliferation of laws and regulations guiding the treatment of mentally ill inmates, changes in the educational services provided for offenders, and a host of other issues have all served to alter the correctional culture in many prisons. Again, prison leaders and managers were left with a dearth of solutions to problems that seemed intractable. Most importantly, what they saw unfold before them was an assault on correctional culture and the traditional ways of doing business. Correctional culture became fragmented along functional lines, and unifying these competing and contentious cultures has been the task of correctional leadership for the past 20 to 40 years. How can the "three cultures" of the prison be unified into one culture, given the difficulties and problems faced by them both individually and collectively?

According to Schein (1997, p. 212), the process of culture formation involves four steps: (1) the founder (leader) has an idea for a new enterprise or vision, (2) the leader identifies other people who share his or her vision, (3) groups are formed to make the vision real, and (4) others who share the vision of the leader and the group are brought into the organization. For correctional leaders, these processes boil down to the following procedures. First, the correctional leader needs to define the core values he or she is trying to advance in the prison. A statement of values becomes extremely important to the functioning of the prison. Second, group consensus and meaning needs to be developed concerning the direction and purpose of the prison. Third, the identification of a correctional vision is needed. In short, the prison has to determine where it wants to be in both the short and the long term. Finally, affecting correctional culture will mean leadership by example. In order for the prison to experience a unification of the three cultures, correctional leaders will have to demonstrate the desired culture to subordinates through their behavior and example.

Correctional Values: Whose Values Are Right?

As stated previously, values are central to effective correctional leadership. At one level, correctional professionals can come to a consensus about what they believe the central values of the prison should be, yet, as suggested earlier, a distinction between *organizational* values and *personal* values is important. Another question concerning the priority of values is of equal importance. For example, do we view prisons primarily as places where the organizational values of security and safety should predominate over other values, such as the treatment of prisoners? Do we not value and hold many diverse expectations for prisons? Can we do it all within prisons, and what does *all* really mean for the correctional leader? More fundamentally, whose values are right, and how do we determine the supremacy of some values over others within the correctional setting? (See the case scenario at end of chapter.)

These are difficult questions for correctional leaders to answer, yet day-to-day pressures force them to select specific values that enable prisons to function. The core values of correctional administrators are tied to the safety and security of the prison staff and the prisoners. This is not to suggest that other organizational values, such as treatment programming, are minimized by prison officials. For many correctional professionals, treatment efforts actually enhance the security values within the prison. They do not see the conflict between security and treatment that the research literature has documented for the past 50 years; instead, they view treatment programming as a legitimate function that buttresses their ability to maintain the security and safety of their institutions.

As an organizational value, then, treatment is important, but it must be understood as a part of the larger prison values of institutional safety and security. As one correctional administrator suggested to one of the authors, "You may be the best social worker, counselor, or therapist in the world, but if your activities in any way jeopardize the security of the prison, you will no longer be here." For this correctional administrator, like many others, such an assessment reflects the values and culture they think should be transmitted by correctional leadership. To support other organizational values within the prison is not an error; it is only an error if those values work toward the dilution of safety and security as the primary values in the prison. Correctional leaders must recognize the primacy of safety and security values if they are to transmit culture and to influence the three cultures within the prison organization.

Correctional Leadership by Example

DiIulio (1987) highlights the importance of leadership visibility in prison when he discusses the management style of former director George Beto of the Texas Department of Corrections. According to DiIulio (1987), Beto exhibited what now is referred to as the infamous "management by walking around" (MBWA). The MBWA style is predicated on the belief that a correctional presence by management and leadership is crucial to the effectiveness of running a prison. In George Beto's case, MBWA meant, in part, showing up at the prison at unannounced times and checking up on employees and inmates. In effect, such a style of management was a form of control that sent a clear message to staff and prisoners that they were going to be held accountable for their actions.

For Beto, the goal was to exercise and maintain control over all who worked and lived in the prison. He was trying to set an *example* of what was expected and of appropriate behavior among all those who lived and worked in the prison. His presence meant something to the prison. From a leadership perspective, Beto was leading by example, and he had very little tolerance for those who would not conform to his directives and views on how the prison was to be run. In this way, his actions engendered specific cultural expectations about the activities and behaviors of staff and prisoners that were congruent with maintaining the safety and security of the prison. Leading by example, therefore, means something very concrete for prison organizations.

Prison managers and correctional officers alike require consistency and an example from those in leadership positions in order for cultural norms to develop. Every correctional staff person must be able to discern what correctional leadership stands for and what practices will be supported and what practices will be frowned upon and dismissed. This understanding lies at the heart of comprehending correctional leadership. Additionally, correctional leaders must not only show by example, but must also demonstrate a continuity in their words and actions. In short, both personal values and organizational values cannot vacillate; there must be some permanency to leaders' values and actions. As one correctional administrator suggested to one of the authors, "Correctional leaders not only must talk the talk, but they must walk the walk, and walk it every day."

Transmitting Culture: Working Together

Working together in the prison means recognizing divergent and diverse interests but then finding a common ground. The tensions and disagreements that make up institutional life are plentiful and normative. Correctional leaders can list numerous examples of situations in which tension, disagreement, and discord have destroyed the morale of prison staff to such a point that nothing productive can be accomplished. Yet, for an effective correctional culture to exist, and for the three dominant cultures to work together, there must be a common understanding of the plurality and diversity of interests in the prison and, more importantly, a recognition that these cultures are working toward the same objectives and goals. How is commonality in purpose achieved in the prison among the three cultures as well as others within the prison?

Commonality in purpose begins with an identification of the values for the prison and the common purpose that emanates from them. A shared meaning of purpose is developed when the three cultural groups in the prison recognize it is in their best interests to work together. It is not uncommon for correctional leaders to espouse the view that working together in the prison means that, for example, correctional officers recognize that treatment staff are their allies in maintaining the security of the prison. Many correctional administrators have developed working relationships across functional lines in their prisons to enhance the safety and orderliness of their institutions. A good example of this is the role that work opportunities and recreational activities play in enhancing the ability of prison staff to preserve institutional order while at the same time working toward the development of skills and behaviors that improve prisoners.

For administrators, managers, and officers, a shared purpose serves to unify potentially divergent and diverse interests in such a way as to move the organization forward. Correctional culture becomes more harmonious, and positive outcomes become more probable. Correctional leadership becomes the linchpin that connects the three cultures and directs them toward a common ground that is respected among those groups and entities that make up the prison organization. Central to the development of this unified culture is the correctional vision. With a correctional vision comes a clear statement of purposes, goals, and objectives and a clear picture of where the prison should be in the future. A construction of a correctional vision is one of the central activities of correctional leadership. So, what is a viable correctional vision, and how does leadership perpetuate such a vision?

Transmitting Values and the Correctional Vision

The transmission of correctional values requires a mechanism. This mechanism is the correctional vision. For effective correctional leadership to exist, correctional leaders must identify where they want to be in the future, while being fully cognizant of both the advantages and limitations of their ideas. They must recognize that there is much uncertainty in any vision they might promulgate, yet their fear of the unknown will not inhibit them from moving forward with a vision for their prison. Nanus (1992) states: "Effective leaders have agendas; they are result oriented. They adopt challenging new visions of what is possible and desirable, communicate their visions, and persuade others to become so committed to these new directions that they are eager to lend their resources and energies to make them happen" (p. 4).

Through the correctional vision of where they want to be in the future, the correctional leadership promotes specific values. In addition, the correctional vision allows leadership to be predictable. Both managers and officers know what the leader stands for and where the prison is headed. Another important product of a correctional vision is that routine is possible, as both correctional staff and inmates have a general understanding of what the leader expects concerning their performance. The specificity of performance is worked out in the daily interactions that make up prison work, but through the correctional vision, both employees and prisoners have a fundamental idea of what the prison is trying to accomplish and where they fit into the larger scheme of operations within the facility.

With a core set of values, a correctional leadership approach that relies on positive examples, the development of group consensus and shared meaning among the three cultures, and an unambiguous correctional vision, the transmission of a unified correctional culture is possible. The actions of correctional leaders in these areas allow for more integration of the diverse correctional interests that define prison culture. It is the transmission and direction of prison culture that ultimately defines effective correctional leadership. As Schein (1997) has noted, nothing is more central to organizational leadership than the ability of leaders to influence culture. We believe this is highly relevant to the prison organization.

TRANSFORMING CULTURE IN PRISON

In 1995, a large department of corrections was hit with a major lawsuit claiming that one of its prisons was engaging in the systematic torture of inmates in the special housing unit (SHU) of the prison. Prisoners were routinely denied medical and psychiatric attention, and physical torture of some prisoners had been documented. In addition, there had been blatant disregard of institutional policy concerning the videotaping of cell extractions.

Many correctional officials across the state who were knowledgeable about the prison, the staff, its operations, and the *culture* of the prison were of the opinion that such problems were predictable, given the prison's current leadership. In fact, at that time correctional officials told one of the authors that many higher officials within the department of corrections and even in the governor's office had expressed concern that the warden of the facility had a reputation for being a heavy-handed administrator who allowed rogue correctional staff to run the prison and reinforce norms and behaviors that were supportive of abusing prisoners; in some cases, the warden had even condoned the mistreatment of prisoners. When the author asked these correctional administrators about solutions to the problems faced by the prison, a view generally expressed was that new leadership was required. These correctional administrators believed the prison would never get a handle on the correctional officer culture without introducing a number of changes, starting with a new warden. The author suggested that the prison needed to experience a transformation of its current culture, especially its correctional officer culture, and that one way to accomplish such a task was to bring in new leadership with differing values and ideas on how the prison should be run.

This solution seems simple enough at one level, but at another level, issues of transformation of prison culture must be addressed within the context of a unique orientation or focus that defines prison organizations. In discussing a change in one of the three dominant prison cultures, it is important to consider the collateral effects of the change on the other two cultures. Cultural transformation in prison requires a comprehension of both the direct and indirect consequences of making changes at the executive level. How will the other cultures respond to such changes?

In the particular prison we have been discussing, replacing the warden would not be enough to solve the prison's problems. Rather, a cultural awareness of how the management culture and the officer culture would react to such a change in the prison's leadership was essential before the transformation of the entire organizational culture could occur. How will the correctional officer culture, for example, respond to the change in the warden, especially given the fact that the warden had been very supportive of the correctional officers in his institution? How will the management culture respond to the change in leadership at the top?

Because of the warden's strong support among correctional officer staff, it was going to be difficult for the department's headquarters to convince the correctional officer culture that a change in the warden's position was necessary. If cultural change was not made in a constructive and conciliatory manner, tension and serious trouble could potentially surface. For the new warden to be effective, he or she would have to convince both managers and correctional officers that changes were necessary and in their best interests. How can this be accomplished among these diverse and competing cultures of managers and officers? This is achieved by a statement of new values and an explanation of why certain values are wrong for the prison. In this case, the dishonesty, brutality, and even illegal behavior by some staff had to be confronted by the new warden and not condoned. The new warden not only had to unequivocally state his or her values, vision, and mission for the prison, but more importantly, he or she also had to identify those values that were wrong for the prison and why they were wrong. Through such an effort, the warden would be appealing to the specific interests of both managers and officers in transforming the prison's culture, as well as trying to unify the fragmented culture that was evident in the prison and a product of the previous warden's decisions and actions.

Value Wars: Whose Values Are Wrong?

So what values are wrong in a prison environment? First we must note the importance of the law—including administrative rules and the legal opinions of courts. The role of the courts in shaping and influencing prison policies and practices has been well documented over the past 35 years (Carroll, 1998). No warden today has not been sued on repeated occasions, and no correctional leader can argue that the influence of the courts on prisons has not been significant to his or her operations. As a value, then, knowing and understanding the law and what is allowable under it is critical for prison organizations. While disagreements may exist concerning the interpretation of the law (see the case scenario at end of chapter), it is fair to conclude that no court today will condone gross violations of prisoners' rights and protections, especially those concerning cruel and unusual punishments and torture.

Organizational values that condone arbitrary and capricious actions rooted in wide-scale violence and brutality against inmates are in no one's best interest. Experienced correctional leaders and managers are aware of the practical problems associated with such behaviors, but more importantly, they know it is just *wrong* for such actions to be condoned by anyone in the prison hierarchy. Again, although correctional leaders may disagree on the purpose, scope, and meaning of the law (i.e., how it is to be interpreted), they have a fundamental understanding that recognizes the legitimacy of the law and its authority to oversee correctional operations; hence, the law has its own force over correctional organizations, but it also has a value that many correctional administrators understand as essential to the operations of correctional institutions. Following the rule of law has both practical and moral import for everyone who works in prisons today.

Organizational values that contradict standards developed by national correctional organizations, such as the American Correctional Association (ACA) and the American Jail Association (AJA), are difficult to justify. These organizations have worked diligently over the past three decades to promulgate practices and standards that represent the "best practices" in the corrections profession. A review of their standards indicates an appeal to values that should undergird all correctional agencies. Values such as fairness, justice, honesty, and integrity, to mention a few, reflect what these professional associations see as the standards upon which we assess the professionalism of the corrections field. In contrast, behaviors and actions that appeal to the ugly side of corrections, founded in violence, deceit, false representations, and misunderstandings, are not consistent with the missions of these associations, nor are they viewed as those values that serve the best interests of correctional professionals.

One example to highlight this point is the use of the term *guard* to describe correctional officers. Both the ACA and the AJA have made public proclamations in opposition to the term *guard*. The ACA and the AJA have attempted to inform the public about the diversity of roles that correctional officers play in protecting the public and promoting constructive change among offenders under their charge. The term *guard* is viewed as pejorative to anyone who has worn an officer uniform and who understands the work performed by correctional officers on a daily basis. As an organizational value, then, by demanding more understanding and respect from those both inside and outside of prison concerning the officer role, we advocate a position that those persons who wear the correctional officer uniform are valuable to the prison. We value who they are as persons and the duties they perform in the prison. Our value of them relates to their diversity and contribution to the effective running of the prison; they are part of the correctional team that makes up the prison organization. In valuing these officers, we demonstrate our commitment to correctional staff and their development. The Wisconsin Department of Corrections states its commitment to correctional staff in the following quotation from its mission statement: "Treating a diverse workforce as valued partners by fostering staff development and effectiveness."

Organizational values that do not treat persons with the respect they deserve and that support behaviors and actions outside the accepted code of conduct for corrections professionals are detrimental to both the individual employee and the prison. Moreover, a clear statement of what we as correctional leaders condone and what we find to be inappropriate or offensive within the prison setting is important, and the definitions of good and bad conduct need to be supported by correctional leaders in both word and deed. Too often, we assume as leaders in organizations that employees know what "doing the right thing" actually entails; nothing could be further from the truth. Correctional employees and offenders need to know what leaders support and what they do not support. The transmission of this information is done through *cultural transformation* of the prison organization. This process begins with a statement of purpose and mission, an articulation of a vision, and other significant processes that serve as "primary embedding mechanisms" in organizations (Schein, 1997).

The Relevance of Transforming Prison Culture

Schein (1997) has noted that organizational leaders can embed and transmit culture in six primary ways: (1) what leaders pay attention to, measure, and control on a regular basis; (2) how leaders react to critical incidents and organizational crises; (3) observed criteria by which leaders allocate scarce resources; (4) deliberate role modeling, teaching, and coaching on the part of the leaders; (5) observed criteria by which leaders allocate rewards and status; and (6) observed criteria by which leaders recruit, select, promote, retire, and excommunicate organizational members. It is obvious in the prison setting that all of these processes are relevant to the transformation of organizational culture and the unification of the three primary cultures under one mission and vision. Too often a lack of attention to the details of these processes is what creates controversy and tension in the prison.

Many correctional administrators have expressed how a leader's lack of attention to detail—with regard to the allocation of scarce resources, for example—can create unwanted tension and bitter antagonism among the competing groups in the prison. For example, suppose allocation of resources is a flash point among the three cultures in the prison. According to many correctional administrators, correctional leaders could minimize much trouble in the prison by clearly articulating where they want to allocate their resources and sticking to that position. As one correctional administrator stated to one of the authors, "Our leadership needs to put its money where its mouth is. If you want to beef up programming in the prison and are willing to use our limited funds to do so, then just say that and do it. If you upset some of the custody staff in the process, so be it. They will just have to adjust, but at least people know where you are coming from. It is the wishy-washy leadership that no one can figure out that upsets me the most."

A correctional leader who seeks to move the prison's three cultures toward acceptance of a new code of conduct among staff needs to make sure that his or her conduct as a leader comports with the expectations defined in the new code. One department of corrections promulgated a "treatment of people" (TOP) program, as well as a code of conduct that respected all employees, to generate more acceptance of diversity in the workforce. When the director of this department introduced the program to employees, it was clear at the outset that the program would fail because of his behavior. In announcing the program, the director was disrespectful toward a particular errant employee. The program was introduced to departmental employees at one of the institutions, and during his opening remarks, the director of the department shouted a profanity at one of his employees that was heard not only among those in attendance at the program's ceremony, but later across the organization. Within days the TOP program was just a joke, created only to placate the governor's staff with very little substance to it. The important point here is that the actions of leaders do matter. Employees and prisoners who see glaring contradictions between the words and deeds of a leader will inevitably kill this person's ability to transmit new values and alter an organization's culture.

Other factors also affect correctional leaders' abilities to change culture. Examples are the policies or procedures put into place to identify and reward good employees and prisoners; how the leaders respond to a crisis such as a disturbance in the prison; how the leaders make subordinates and prisoners aware of what they will be controlling, measuring, and observing in their behaviors; and the processes the leaders put into place to hire, retain, promote, and remove employees from the prison organization. As Schein (1997) suggests, each of these processes has a profound effect on the degree to which a leader can embed and create an organizational culture. Such processes become even more problematic in a prison organization due to the competing nature of the three cultures that make up the prison environment. As suggested earlier, the primary purpose of correctional leadership is to unify these disparate cultural groups such that the mission and vision of the prison is possible.

Cultural transformation in the prison, therefore, centers around the ability of correctional leaders to bring together the divergent interests of the three cultures and identify a common ground and purpose in the prison. Effective correctional leadership cannot be understood without focusing on the processes and practices that will bring these three cultures together. The primary question for correctional leadership is the following: *What issues define the common purpose among the three cultures within the prison?* A secondary concern relates to the processes by which this common purpose is defined.

Cultural Transformation and the Three Cultures in Prison

For many, the prison's central purpose is the maintenance of order, security, and control of prisoners. While the academic debate concerning the efficacy of treatment and how and under what conditions prisons are able to intervene in the lives of offenders continues, for correctional professionals in the prison there is no lack of consensus about the prison's primary purpose. For these practical-minded individuals, the purpose that unifies the prison centers around the safety and security that the prison can provide for both prisoners and staff alike. Anything that enhances the likelihood of the environment being more safe and secure will serve the purpose of unifying the three cultures in prisons. Anything that detracts from such a purpose will serve to fragment the three cultures.

Efforts toward transforming correctional culture must be directed toward an awareness of the fundamental purpose of the prison: to ensure the safety and security of prisoners and staff. Correctional leadership that engages such a view goes a long way toward unifying the sometimes discordant interests reflected by the three cultures within the prison. A common purpose in prison means an identification and allegiance to the core practices that make the prison a safe place. Under such a broad definition of purpose, there is much room for the three cultures within the prison to function and adapt to one another.

An excellent example to highlight this point is the relationship that exists between custody personnel and treatment staff within prisons. The accepted and traditional view has been that the "treatment-custody" conflict makes prisons an unsuitable place for prisoners to be rehabilitated. In the words of the historian David Rothman (1980), "when custody and treatment conflicted [in prisons], custody always won." This view, however, is rather shortsighted and lacks insight concerning how treatment and custody functions within prisons do not have to be conflicting and contrastive; instead, these two major activities can be complementary. Correctional professionals across the country have known for decades that a safe and secure prison is best achieved when the outlets for inmate expression are enhanced. In other words, treatment programs and other such initiatives are not inimical to the long-term stability and safety of the prison. Rather, such programming actually enhances the security of the institution. Security personnel have expressed this position for many years, and prisoners have consistently expressed the same view when it comes to their interests in treatment programming and other outlets in the prison.

Correctional leaders committed to the transformation of prison culture must pay attention to those issues or themes that will bring together the three cultures of the prison. Setting an expectation that the fundamental purpose of the prison will be the maintenance of a safe and secure environment will go a long way toward solidifying the three cultures in the prison. Being aware of other issues that are indicative of a common thread that ties the prison's cultures together will also assist the leader in transforming the larger organizational culture. The primary issue that must be addressed by correctional leaders is how their vision assists or hinders the transformation of the organizational culture in the prison.

Visionary Correctional Leadership and Transforming Culture

For the visionary correctional leader, the necessity of adopting a vision that recognizes the importance of safety and security as a unifying cultural element cannot be overstated. Too often correctional leaders publicly promulgate correctional visions that are too far removed from the central purpose and reality of the prison, that is, institutional safety, security, and control, as identified by the three cultures. Correctional leadership means envisioning and implementing policies and practices that make the prison a better place, as evidenced by fewer assaults on inmates and staff, greater opportunities for correctional staff and prisoners to develop, and fewer tensions and competition among the three cultures in the prison, to mention just a few of the things that make a prison a better place. Visionary correctional leadership sees the opportunity for the prison to function more effectively and toward the attainment of the prison's goals of ensuring a safe and secure environment.

As a consequence of the correctional leader's vision, the three cultures should be integrated in such a fashion that tangible products of the transformation process of the larger, correctional culture are evident. Not only should there be reduced rates of violence in the prison, for example, but changes in the climate of the prison also should become more apparent. Correctional staff will be more committed to the prison. Their efforts and investments in the prison should increase. Better relations between correctional staff and correctional administrators should be evidenced. Fewer vitriolic and counterproductive interactions between staff and management should occur. Moreover, the prisoner culture should become more stable and less fragmented. Correctional leaders who send the message through staff that the prison will do everything practically possible to control violence among inmates and between inmates and staff will do much to improve the conditions for a majority of prisoners. A *cultural norm* will be developed and adhered to by the prisoner culture that violence will not be tolerated.

The long-term effects of visionary correctional leadership are plentiful. To start, visionary correctional leadership sets the moral tone for the prison. It defines what the prison is about, and also where the prison should be. In addition, visionary correctional leadership identifies the expectations that correctional leaders have for both prisoners and staff. Through the vision, the three cultures can respond to specific norms and ideas based on how the correctional leader expects them to perform their duties. Too often leaders and managers fail to provide the proper guidance and direction to subordinates in the area of performance of duties. For the correctional leader, the daily interactions of the three cultures of the prison are not significant; this concern is the purview of management. Correctional leadership, however, is responsible for defining the contours of the vision that correctional managers are responsible for operationalizing. Both are critical to the transformation of correctional culture. Without the vision, correctional management is left with a void, one that must be filled by those in positions of leading the prison.

The final benefit of visionary correctional leadership is the empowerment it provides to employees within the organization. Through an agreed-upon vision, correctional leaders ensure that the energies and activities of the correctional staff are directed toward an effort that they support. The correctional leader is only the midwife of the correctional vision for the prison. To make it tangible and real, correctional staff must pursue the vision, nurture and develop it, and carry it forward. It is through their involvement and commitment to the vision that the larger correctional culture is influenced and ultimately the three cultures of the prison are cemented. Many who write about visionary leadership see this as boiling down to empowerment for employees (Nanus, 1992). As they carry the correctional vision forward, managers and officers recognize that it is not just the prison's vision, but their own vision as well. For the larger correctional culture, the effect of visionary correctional leadership is the solidification of the three cultures in the prison around a common purpose, a purpose recognized as legitimate and worthwhile for *all* members to show allegiance to in the prison.

CULTURAL CHANGE AND ORGANIZATIONAL POLITICS

We would be remiss if we did not discuss the influence that cultural change has on organizational politics within prisons. Similar to any other organization, prisons exhibit highly particularized and idiosyncratic patterns of interaction that are rooted in political power and political aspirations among participants. For cultural change to happen within prisons, there must be an awareness of the implications of such change on the politics of the organization. Different groups employ the political processes of the prison to advance their own interests. When cultural change occurs within prisons, there is a discernable shift in the political power and interests that were served by the old ways of doing business.

Cultural change in the prison, especially radical cultural change, produces significant alterations of power bases. Some destabilization of prison operations is likely, at least for a time. This destabilization of the prison is a necessary part of the process of adjusting to the new cultural norms being transmitted by the prison's leadership. In some cases, people and positions will be shuffled and removed due to the change, but in the long run, this is in the best interests of those who represent the new "status quo" in the prison. For managers, officers, and administrators within the three cultures of the prison, things will change, but usually not so significantly that these groups cannot adjust and assimilate the new expectations of leaders into their ways of doing business in the prison. Nevertheless, cultural change in the prison will bring new, as well as old, issues to the surface, so tension and disharmony are to some extent probable outcomes. In seeking a new set of norms and expectations to guide the prison, effective correctional leadership will produce change. In some cases, those with extant interests will be upset, while others will see the change as an opportunity to promote their own agendas and interests under new leadership.

For correctional leadership, the integration of the cultures of managers, officers, and other administrators will be formidable, but not impossible. Effective correctional leadership recognizes that cultural change in the prison begins with a creation of a mission statement, a declaration of a discernable vision for the prison, and an adherence to some core values that define leadership character and purpose. The task for prison leadership is to accomplish these objectives while still being cognizant of organizational politics. Each of the three cultures in the prison will view the vision from the perspective of its importance to their own interests. Correctional leaders who are unaware of or insensitive to the interests of the three dominant cultures in developing the vision will have a tough road to walk, since their chance of gaining support from members of all three cultures will be low. This is, again, why correctional leadership is so crucial. For the correctional vision to have a chance, correctional leaders must show members of all three cultures that such a vision is consistent with their own interests and values and that an integration of the three cultures into *one* organizational culture will serve the prison well.

CORRECTIONAL CULTURE: A CONCLUDING COMMENT

In this chapter and in Chapter 5, we identified why we think the transformation of prison culture is so relevant to correctional leadership. We focused primarily on the internal stakeholders and the three cultures of the prison. In the concluding chapter of this book, we will focus on strategies for correctional success, as well as obstacles and future considerations for correctional leaders. The external environment of the prison and certain public and private interests have a major role in prison leadership as we begin this new century. The environment of the 21st century prison will force leaders to begin to address not only the three cultures inside their institutions, but also those critical actors and entities outside the prison who have a significant role in shaping the practice of correctional leadership. How correctional leaders respond to these external persons or groups may be the most important test they will face during this century.

CASE SCENARIO   *Prisoner Litigation and Differing Prison Cultures*

The Tuberville prison had a long history of problems with a fringe element of the correctional officer corp. Many officers within the department of corrections knew that being sent to Tuberville meant being relegated to one of the state's worst prisons. The prison, known as TP, had a history of critical incidents involving correctional officers, some of which were perceived to be very negative by the media, particular legislators, and the courts. In fact, an appellate court had ruled against TP and the warden when it found the prison in noncompliance with court orders to improve prisoners' access to the courts, even though the prison and the department of corrections viewed its inmate law library and access policies and procedures to the courts to be in full compliance with current law, and in particular the Prison Litigation Reform Act (PLRA) of 1996 which placed restrictions on inmate lawsuits, filing times, and the number of times a prisoner could sue a prison and a department of corrections.

Nevertheless, TP was in trouble. The correctional officer union ran with their interpretation of the PLRA to mean that prisoners couldn't file as many lawsuits against the officers and other correctional staff as they did in the past. For them, PLRA was about time; it gave officers more authority to control inmate movement, and from their perspective, the legislation was a victory for correctional officers because it reinforced their belief that many inmate lawsuits were "bullshit" and a hindrance to them in the performance of their duties. In practice, the implementation policy in the PLRA guidelines issued by the depart-

ment of corrections was clear: the determination of when and how inmates should be allowed to file appeals was to be controlled by the central office; the PLRA did not mean that inmates were to be treated differently by officers concerning their involvement in lawsuits and filings against the prison or the department of corrections. Yet, some vocal officers who were active union members seized the PLRA as an opportunity to change what they perceived to be a liberal policy allowing inmates too much access to the prison's law library.

For other correctional staff and prisoners, the law library was viewed as a positive part of the prison's larger strategy to educate prisoners about their rights and, specifically, as a venue by which inmates could file legal claims when the institution's own grievance mechanisms were unable to provide the needed relief. In fact, the prison had been able to get badly needed medical equipment and more medical staff as the result of a lawsuit filed by an inmate. Many institutional managers, prisoners, and correctional staff secretly supported the lawsuit and the inmate who filed it as a way to secure resources from the state when the state made it clear that it was not going to improve the medical services in the prison.

The warden of the facility realized that there were competing correctional cultures in her institution. The correctional officers, as represented by the union, had one view of the inmate-access-to-the-courts issue. Correctional managers had another view. Prisoners had a view similar to that of the managers, but for different reasons.

Case Scenario continued

In the middle of these differing views was the warden who saw herself as a person who was trying to unify these disparate perspectives into one organizational culture. What was she to do?

Case Scenario Questions

1. What are some strategies you would propose to the warden to address the apparent conflict that exists among the competing cultures within the prison on this issue of access to the courts?

2. Identify the competing cultures in this scenario. What is both positive and problematic about viewing prisons as places where there are competing cultures?

3. What values are implicitly or explicitly being portrayed among the different prison cultures in the scenario? Are there any "right" or "wrong" values in this scenario in relation to the different prison cultures?

REFERENCES

Carroll, L. (1998). *Lawful order: A case study of correctional crisis and reform*. New York: Garland.

DiIulio, J. (1987). *Governing prisons: A comparative study of correctional management*. New York: Free Press.

Farkas, M. A., & Manning, P. K. (1997). The occupational culture of policing and correctional work. *Journal of Crime and Justice, 22*(2), 51–68.

Glaser, D. (1995). *Preparing convicts for law-abiding lives: The pioneering penology of Richard A. McGee*. Albany, NY: State University of New York Press.

Houston, J. (1999). *Correctional management: Functions, skills, and systems* (2nd ed.). Chicago: Nelson-Hall.

Irwin, J. (1980). *Prisons in turmoil*. Boston: Little, Brown.

Jacobs, J. (1977). *Stateville: The penitentiary in mass society*. Chicago: University of Chicago Press.

Nanus, B. (1992). *Visionary leadership*. San Francisco: Jossey-Bass.

Rothman, D. (1980). *Conscience and convenience: The asylum and its alternatives in progressive America*. Boston: Little, Brown.

Schein, E. (1997). *Organizational culture and leadership* (2nd ed.). San Francisco: Jossey-Bass.

CORRECTIONAL LEADERSHIP AND THE FUTURE

CORRECTIONAL LEADERSHIP: THE 21ST CENTURY

Correctional leadership will face many challenges in the 21st century. Among them will be a ballooning inmate population, a serious labor shortage of correctional officers, a more diverse correctional workforce, infinite demands and finite resources, and greater accountability to a diversity of stakeholders. All these challenges have at their core the management of people, particularly the management of human relationships. As we emphasized in our introduction, the essence of correctional leadership is the *art of developing, nurturing, and maintaining these relationships*. This will become even more critical in the 21st century than in the past. The effective leader must develop the skills to work with people—staff, offenders, and the many internal and external stakeholders. Human relationships in the organization must be elevated to a prominent place in strategic planning for the future. This chapter will discuss the challenges facing leadership and explore strategies to help leaders in their relations with correctional staff and in their interface with the many significant stakeholders and powerful lobbies in the external environment.

An expanding inmate population will continue to challenge prison officials. At midyear 2000, U.S. prisons and jails incarcerated 1,931,859 persons (Beck & Karberg, 2001). These numbers are expected to increase exponentially not only as a result of crime trends, but also, more importantly, as a result of mandatory sentencing, habitual offender statutes, sentence enhancements directed toward gun-related and drug-related crimes, and the abolition of parole in many states. The total inmate population is projected to reach 2.2 million by the year 2005 (Beck & Karberg, 2001). The growing number of elderly, mentally ill, and other special needs inmates is also a daunting prospect for correctional leaders.

Another challenge emerges from an analysis of labor force projections for the 21st century. The American labor force is expected to increase more slowly than at any other time since the 1930s (Loden & Rosener, 1991), yet the employment need for correctional officers is expected to increase 36% or more, much faster than the average for all occupations (Bureau of Labor Statistics, 2000). The construction of new prisons and the expansion of existing facilities will create a demand for many new correctional officers. Over the next 10 years, an estimated 25,300 officer openings will need to be filled each year to minimally meet the staffing needs of correctional institutions (Kiekbusch, 2001). Of this number, 14,800 will be new positions, and the remainder will be vacancies in existing positions due to turnover and retirement (Kieckbusch, 2001). The continued reliance on incarceration as the primary form of punishment in the United States will help make these projections a reality.

Changing organizational demographics will present still another dilemma for correctional administration. Labor force diversity will continue to increase in the 21st century. Corrections, along with many other occupations, will face a dramatically different labor market in terms of race, ethnicity, gender, and age. One third of new workers will be minorities, especially Blacks and Hispanics, due to immigration and high birth rates (Loden & Rosener, 1991). Approximately 450,000 more immigrants are expected to enter the United States yearly through the end of the 21st century (Loden & Rosener, 1991: p. 10). The labor force participation of women will continue to rise (Fullerton, 1999). Age will also become a factor with the so-called "baby boomers" (roughly ages 35–54) remaining in the workforce in full force combined with a decreasing pool of younger workers (ages 25–34) (Loden & Rosener, 1991). The age group of workers 55 and older is identified as having not only the fastest rate of population growth, but also the greatest increases in labor force participation. With the population projected to continue aging so rapidly, the median age of the labor force in the year 2008 will be 40.7 (Fullerton, 1999). Leaders will be called upon to integrate and accommodate older, more diverse individuals into their workforce. Their people skills will be tested as they are charged with the primary responsibility for developing and promoting relationships with and among correctional personnel who may be quite different from the once predominantly white, male staff.

Correctional leaders will also be confronted with the need to manage their relationships with many internal and external audiences in a time of declining resources, labor shortages, limited funds and infinite demands, and shifting politics. They will be held more accountable legally, contractually, and fiscally to these varied groups. Court decisions will continue to affect policies, procedures, and standards of care for inmates. Huge correctional budgets have drawn legislatures into trying to micromanage the system (Stojkovic, Kalinich, & Klofas, 1998). Leaders must acknowledge the political nature of their role and become more attentive and responsive to political and economic processes.

STRATEGIES FOR CORRECTIONAL SUCCESS: THE 21ST CENTURY

The Importance of Values and Vision

Solutions to meet the challenges of correctional leaders require that such leaders take a more proactive, people-oriented role than they have in the past. Leaders must not only state clearly what their values are and how they fit into their vision for the organization, but they also must actively demonstrate their beliefs. Leader behavior in terms of how values are practiced in front of employees is an important way to embed and transmit culture. Visible actions communicate assumptions and values to other organizational members (Schein, 1992, p. 240). "Leader modeling" is one deliberate way to coalesce divergent values and assumptions into a shared understanding of interactions and relationships among employees. With leader modeling, the leader effectively and consistently models the desired behaviors, thus giving other members "permission" to exhibit these behaviors as well (Banner & Gagne, 1995).

Commitment to the values and vision of the prison organization is demonstrated through the actions of the leaders. The warden who is highly visible in the prison exemplifies a belief in firsthand knowledge of the job and accessibility to staff. The warden who consistently seeks the input of staff regarding their responsibilities shows them that they are participants in running the institution and that their opinions are valued. These behaviors display to followers that they have the support of the highest level of management (Bass & Avolio, 1994, p. 45).

What leaders pay attention to is another powerful cultural embedding mechanism (Schein, 1992, p. 231). What prison wardens notice, question, and reward positively or negatively reflects their principles and beliefs. Desired values and behaviors may be further ingrained by corresponding tangible and intangible rewards. As Schein (1992) asserts, "Whereas the message initially gets across in the daily behavior of the leader, it is judged in the long run by whether the important rewards are allocated consistently with that daily behavior" (p. 243). Observed rewards, such as delegation of more authority, a more challenging job assignment, or a leadership role on a project, instill the idea that certain behaviors and values are the goals to strive for. Praise for a staff member who has been observed acting toward an inmate in a manner that is consistent with the goals and mission of the organization sends a powerful message of how to treat inmates. Even a casual remark by a leader can be an effective reinforcer of desired behavior.

Employee Empowerment

Employee morale and job stress will continue to be significant issues for the correctional administration in the 21st century. Among the major stressors identified by correctional officers are a lack of participation in decision making (Lindquist & Whitehead, 1986; Lombardo, 1981; Patterson, 1992), a feeling of powerlessness (Lombardo, 1981), lack of support by administrators and coworkers (Cullen, Link, Wolfe, & Frank, 1985), and role ambiguity with no clear expectations concerning job performance (Pogrebin & Atkins, 1982). Workers who feel empowered have a positive effect on both the organization and individuals through increased job satisfaction and work productivity/effectiveness and a decreased propensity to leave the organization (Koberg, Boss, Senjem, & Goodman, 1999). Correctional leaders can play a central role in the empowerment of their employees and in the transformation to a culture that is supportive of empowerment. Empowering employees refers to leaders influencing employees to become more active and self-sufficient in realizing the goals of the organization (Herrenkohl, Judson, & Heffner, 1999).

The organizational and management literature contains a wide variety of conceptual and operational definitions of empowerment. For our purposes, we will conceptualize empowerment as having four basic dimensions or elements: (1) an understanding of and shared belief in the organizational mission and goals; (2) an understanding and recognition of the central values, beliefs, and norms of the organization; (3) an influence with colleagues and leadership regarding job responsibilities and work performance; and (4) a culture supportive of employee participation, growth, and initiative.

The shared belief in the organizational mission and goals concerns correctional staff understanding clearly where the organization is headed and what the goals are. Employees are empowered because their efforts are directed toward a specific purpose. Employee empowerment results in a commitment to the mission and goals and a sense of responsibility in carrying them out. Leaders must forge an organization with a clearly formulated and articulated mission and clearly identified goals and objectives; however, they must do so in concert with employees. Together leaders and employees must develop categories of shared meaning that organize their perceptions and thoughts, filtering out what is unimportant, while focusing on what is important (Schein, 1992, p. 71). This reduces uncertainty, role conflict, and dissonance among the organization's members.

Employees are also more likely to feel empowered in organizations when they can influence coworkers, leadership, and their work situation. Influence over the work situation concerns the ability of an employee to effect changes in several areas, including safety, productivity, social relations, and work culture. Group decision making, trust, and the sharing of responsibilities and problems enhance members' feelings of self-determination and competency (Koberg, Boss, Senjem, & Goodman, 1999). Having others, particularly leaders, listen and consider their opinions creates in employees a feeling of empowerment and a perception of support from the administration and coworkers. Effective leaders work together with their correctional staff to solve problems and develop open communication and a level of trust.

Correctional Leadership and Strategic Planning

Strategic planning is essentially long-range planning that involves envisioning and forecasting the future needs of the correctional facility. An essential part of the planning involves assessing the current social, economic, and political conditions, population demographics, and labor market trends for indications of future conditions or concerns. Estimating the impact of prospective problems and the impact of decisions or solutions is also critical to decision making. Planners must institute a series of alternative solutions for the problems, taking into account present and future constraints (Stojkovic, Kalinich, & Klofas, 1998).

As mentioned earlier, there are clear indicators of critical junctures ahead for leadership. The ever-increasing offender population is a persistent concern for correctional administrators. Leadership will be charged with planning to house these inmates and to accommodate their needs, as well as the needs of the rising numbers of aging, mentally ill, and chronically ill inmates. Kiekbusch (2001) argues that prison officials should assume a more proactive role when confronting external stakeholders about operational, technological, and staffing concerns. He contends that they should exert their influence by explaining the impact of the large numbers of offenders on the correctional system. As part of their strategic plan, leaders can advocate to legislators and politicians for less reliance on incarceration as the principal punishment mechanism. They can promote the use of alternative sanctions for less serious offenders. In other words, leadership can play a more active part in determining the future of corrections.

The proliferation of prisons under current correctional policy necessitates the hiring of adequate staff for these facilities. As even more prisons are built, the anticipated labor shortage of correctional officers will rise to the fore. The prison leader must anticipate this critical need for staff, devise alternative sources of recruitment, and develop creative strategies to attract and retain individuals.

Research by Patenaude (2001) pointed to low rates of pay and inadequate employee benefits as significant issues affecting the retention of correctional officers. Corrections can no longer afford an annual turnover rate ranging from 16.2% to 40% (Jurik & Winn, 1987). Changing this situation may involve efforts to win legislative support for restructuring correctional officer pay scales, developing financial incentives for employees to remain in corrections, and improving employee benefits (Patenaude, 2001). Recruitment strategies must incorporate labor trend data, and leaders should consider recruiting from diverse groups. Leadership itself must include women and men from all age groups and racial and ethnic groups in order to be competitive with other occupations and industries (Silverman, 2001).

Strategic planning must also include efforts to make correctional work more challenging and interesting. Changing and shaping the work culture must be a part of any strategic management plan. The traditional work culture was described in Chapter 4 as bureaucratic, hierarchical, rigid, and inflexible; the emphasis was on uniformity in dress and action, routines, and order, and employees were seen largely as automatons following rules, policies, and directives. This culture must be changed to meet the challenges facing correctional leaders in the 21st century. Strategies of empowerment must be incorporated in present and future plans. Correctional employees of this century must be able to make decisions and act to promote the mission and goals of the organization. They must be able to communicate and work collaboratively to define a culture that embraces challenge, innovation, employee participation, and inclusion.

Correctional Leadership and Organizational Culture: A Comment on Diversity

Managing the workforce in the 21st century will present both a challenge and an opportunity. The challenge will be to reconcile the different perspectives of organizational members. Leadership must understand that there may be only one organization, but there are multiple realities shaped by the different experiences and perceptions of women, people of color, and white men (Bond & Pyle, 1998). The empowerment of employees and the transformation of culture are affected by the characteristics of both the organization or work group and the individuals in it (Koberg, Boss, Senjem, & Goodman, 1999). Individual workers have unique perspectives and understandings of human interactions and communication among organizational members. They may have stereotypical notions or ethnocentric views of how one should behave. These attitudes are influenced by many factors, including socialization, socioeconomic background, gender, race, ethnicity, and even age. These differing value systems and meanings can result in misunderstandings, conflict, and fragmentation of the organization into several subgroups.

The opportunity is for leadership to foster an organizational culture that truly values diversity among its members and capitalizes on that diversity. The culture must be supportive and open to the ideas and insights of an increasingly diverse workforce. The correctional leader must work aggressively to remove all practical and cultural barriers to the hiring and full integration of minorities, women, and older individuals, not only as a matter of legal, political, and social importance, but also out of economic necessity (Loden & Rosener, 1991). Managing employees requires more than the formulation of policies and procedures to ensure fair and equitable treatment; it also involves the development of a work culture that promotes the inclusion of all employees as part of a work group. Leaders need to recognize that even though formal policies may be in place, informal processes and practices can keep women and people of color at the margins and maintain their marginality through the creation of an unwelcoming, noninclusive culture (Bond & Pyle, 1998).

Leaders must promote effective intercultural and interpersonal communication among employees through initiatives to develop these areas of communication. They must use their communication skills to learn about their employees' values, motivations, styles of communication, attitudes, and needs (Henderson, 1994, p. 195). A supportive culture encourages employee participation from all its members, facilitates respect for one another among diverse employees, and values individual employee contributions. Developing such a culture requires leaders to have strong interpersonal skills, an awareness and understanding of cultural differences, and knowledge of how to foster and support individual growth within the context of the group. It will take a long-term commitment from correctional leadership to transform the work culture to one that is aligned with the vision, mission, and values of the organization.

OBSTACLES AND FUTURE CONSIDERATIONS FOR CORRECTIONAL LEADERS

We conclude this book by examining some of the issues that will be at the correctional forefront in the next 25 years and will have a significant impact on correctional leadership. We will begin by looking at the problematic nexus between private companies and public entities in the corrections field. For the correctional leader of the 21st century, no other issue will have a more immediate or profound impact on prison operations—and therefore correctional leadership—than the role private entities and differing strategies will play in the delivery of correctional services.

In addition, we will examine the always volatile interactions among governors, legislators, and correctional unions and correctional leadership. We contend that effective 21st century correctional leadership will require more direct attention and effort on the part of prison leaders to the intricacies of politics and the political process. For effective prison leadership to exist, there will have to be a conscious and coordinated plan on the part of leaders to become involved and more politically astute concerning the political process and how it impacts and influences correctional operations.

Moreover, we will discuss the importance of research and evaluation to prison leadership, especially the connection between research and policy development. Finally, we will offer some future correctional scenarios to highlight the primary theme of this book: Correctional leadership is really about organizational culture—its creation, implementation, and perpetuation.

Private Involvement and Public Concerns: The Future of Corrections

The landscape of correctional history has been strewn with both positive and negative experiences of private involvement in service delivery within prisons. For many decades in the 20th century, private vendors provided a host of contracted services to prisons, including but not limited to the following: food delivery, medical services, and treatment alternatives. Those who have been involved in the delivery of correctional services for a long period of time know that the question has never been whether private entities should provide correctional services; instead, the issue has been the *degree* to which private involvement has been central to the operations of prisons. Most pressing for correctional leaders of the 21st century is how far we will go in allowing private interests to become involved in the operations of correctional facilities.

State and federal governmental entities have engaged in a myriad of contractual relationships with private vendors for the delivery of correctional services for many years. Where the discussion has been somewhat altered is, again, the degree to which private involvement has pervaded what was traditionally the domain of the public sector in the corrections field. For correctional leadership, the primary issues are not only of a qualitative and quantitative nature (i.e., what prison operations should be privatized, and how many), but they also, and more importantly, reflect a concern about both the substance and the style of how prisons are to be managed and led. The future of correctional leadership in prisons will hinge on the degree to which private ideas on the management and leadership of large organizations have relevance for those who run publicly subsidized prisons. Addressing this concern will be the central issue defining the relationship between private entities and public organizations in the immediate future. The concern, however, is more than how many prisons will be built and who will manage and lead them; it is *how* the 21st century prison will run and toward what it will *aim*.

Technical questions concerning costs and efficacy will become overshadowed by concerns designed to assess what we want to achieve in the 21st century prison and what methods we will employ to achieve our aims. From a correctional leadership perspective, the relevant issues center around how the traditional, hierarchically organized structure of a prison is able to respond to the aims we have defined as the central purpose of a prison. As stated, the primary purpose of the prison has been the maintenance of security and control of the prisoner population; and from an organizational cultural perspective, effective correctional leadership must engender a culture that recognizes this mission and attaches importance to a vision that reinforces employee empowerment and involvement in the realization of this mission.

It is here that the methodology of the private sector may be of value to those who manage and lead correctional institutions. Private involvement becomes critical when the methods and approaches to leading and managing large organizations that are so well documented in the literature become relevant to public organizations such as prisons (Rainey, 1997). The future of correctional leadership will be predicated, in part, on how well correctional leaders and managers are able to recognize that the traditionally defined hierarchy of presumed control through centralized decision making, rigid policies and procedures, and the sacrosanct belief in the power of the ever-present "chain of command" will not be able to address the demands and expectations of the 21st century prison. In fact, many writers have criticized that classical structure of prison hierarchy as limited and never really providing the great control and order to prisons that it was supposed to provide (Gilbert, 1999). Private involvement in prisons will revolve around challenging traditional views on prison organization, structure, and ways of doing business.

The debate about how best to manage and lead the prison will continue. We suggest that for private involvement in prison to have any meaning for prison leadership in the 21st century, a questioning of traditional leadership methods has to occur. The primary aim of prisons is clear: to provide safe and secure institutions where productive change is possible among prisoners. This aim is best achieved through the creation of an organizational culture that values employees, empowers them, and works toward the integration of the three dominant cultures of the prison. This is the purview of correctional leadership.

The discussion of correctional leadership, however, will have to become more broad-based and include the contribution that private involvement can provide. We know that the movement in public sector organizations toward a recognition of differing approaches to leading and managing people in large organizations has been significantly influenced by those interested in the privatization of public works. Such promotions potentially have both positive and negative ramifications for the operations of governmental agencies such as prisons. Nevertheless, the change in approach, structure, and focus is intriguing for those interested in improving correctional leadership and applying ideas learned in other settings. Prison administrators have adopted parochial and narrow views on how to run prisons for too long; a new set of eyes is needed. The literature in business, political science, management, and psychology (to mention only a few areas) provides a new foundation upon which effective correctional leadership ideas can emerge. The view of an organization as being composed of different cultures is particularly revealing and useful to prison leaders, but the literature also contains a wealth of other ideas and programs that can be useful to correctional leaders.

The future of correctional leadership will be one in which the proper creation, implementation, and perpetuation of culture will be the standard upon which correctional leaders are assessed. These new correctional leaders cannot be bound by the structures, ceremonies, and myths of the old prison, since they will be assessed on how well they lead and on the results they produce. No longer will growth and how well they deal with growth be the simple measures upon which they are evaluated, as in the 1980s and 1990s. Instead, correctional leaders will be expected to be results-oriented. In the words of the former director of the Federal Bureau of Prisons, Michael Quinlan, as cited by Stupak (1999): "Growth for the sake of growth is the etiology of the cancer cell, and that means organizational death. There is only one kind of growth that is sustainable, and that is quality growth based on tough choices, measured outcomes, and cost-benefit tradeoffs" (p. 444).

For the correctional leader of the future, addressing these "tough choices" will require a full array of options, leadership approaches, and resources. Therefore, the nexus between the private world and the public domain of corrections can only become more firm. The relationship created by correctional leaders with the private sector will become more evident and central to their operations in the future. The prison to a large degree will become more permeable, and its traditional ways of doing business will be questioned and, in some cases, replaced by more sophisticated approaches and structures that will make the prison a more safe, secure, and productive place for both prisoners and employees.

For the effective correctional leader, the private-public connection will be an opportunity; for the correctional traditionalist, this connection will be a threat. How the situation will play itself out over the first two decades of the 21st century is hard to predict, but the message is clear: The private-public distinction will need to fade away if correctional leadership is to flourish and prison leaders are to promote an organizational culture that will enhance the chances of prisoners to lead law-abiding lives and correctional employees to flourish and become committed to careers in correctional work.

Governors, Legislatures, Unions, and Correctional Leadership

"Politics is the lifeblood of administration," stated the political scientist Norton Long more than 60 years ago. For correctional leadership, recognition and acceptance of this view is critical. All correctional leaders recognize how politics influences both the internal and external operations of prisons, yet for many, skillful manipulation of political processes, particularly politics played in the external world of the prison, is rare. As suggested previously, knowledge of the political domain in which correctional leaders find themselves is necessary to effective correctional leadership. But, for many correctional leaders, how to effectively work the subtle nuances of the political terrain in which they find themselves is oftentimes neither discussed nor analytically addressed as part of their leadership regimen.

For many correctional leaders, politics is simply an unavoidable dirty word and practice, something to be frowned upon and left to others to address. Such a strategy, however, is deadly and counterproductive in advancing the interests and concerns of prisons. Most important, the end result of such a strategy is the threat of being viewed as weak and incompetent to those who matter in the political arena, for example, those who control budgetary decisions that affect prisons. Therefore, for correctional leadership to be effective in the future, significant political entities need to be identified and cultivated. There are many potentially important political groups that may influence how departments of corrections will function and what type of leadership will prevail. We believe, however, that there are three primary political entities that have an important say in the type of correctional leadership found within departments of corrections: governors, legislatures, and unions.

These three groups are by no means the only significant political actors that may influence correctional leadership. Some would say that the courts, for example, are another group with a large degree of control and influence over correctional leaders. We do not deny the validity of such a claim, but for our purposes, we see governors, legislatures, and unions as being more critical to correctional leadership on a day-to-day basis. Although other groups like the courts are relevant and important to effective correctional leadership, in most jurisdictions they are not as directly involved in laying the foundation for effective correctional leadership.

Governors. For governors, correctional leadership is both a blessing and an anathema. On the one hand, governors can use correctional issues and crime to further advance their own political agendas; on the other hand, the business of corrections is expensive and is constantly under the scrutiny of critics who view it as too expensive of a venture given the return on the dollar. In the middle of this tension between political interest and financial concern is the correctional leader. The expression of this tension is most felt by directors or secretaries of corrections across the states who are accountable to governors directly, since most are appointed by governors. But, as one former director of a large department of corrections commented, "Political heat from governors is the name of the game when you run such a large public agency, but the people who really feel the heat are those underneath me. . . . In our department, it is the wardens who really get squeezed by the governor's office, especially when something goes wrong at their prisons." As political actors, governors have used correctional issues and correctional leaders to propose their projects and to take the heat when critics have confronted them.

Being in the political hot seat as a correctional leader is not the concern so much as the degree to which correctional leaders have to passively accept the ideas and programs of governors when they know, in many cases, that such initiatives will do nothing to protect society, reduce crime, protect victims, or enhance prisoner adjustment. Earlier we mentioned how governors have stepped into both the management and leadership of prisons during the past 20 years to a degree that is unprecedented and unparalleled in our history. This fact by itself is not demonstrative of anything, but in tandem with the abdication-of-leadership behavior by many correctional professionals, it has caused many of the problems (e.g., overcrowding, poor treatment efforts, and demoralized and overburdened staff) that the 21st century prison faces.

At the forefront of the current problems lies the ineffective correctional leadership that has not spoken truth to power vis-à-vis a governor or executive concerning correctional matters. Too many correctional leaders deny their responsibility to productively influence governors and their staffs by communicating with them on what makes sense within prisons. One example of this is the situation described previously where the governor wanted to initiate a "giveback" program whereby prisoners would lose most of their privileges, such as weightlifting and other recreational activities. The director lamented about many things concerning this new program but was particularly concerned about the practical difficulties he was going to face with wardens, correctional staff, unions, and the prisoners when implementing it.

One of the authors discussed the give-back program with the director. Considering that some of the perceived "amenities" selected to be given back by the department were integral to the prisons' functioning and long-term objectives and goals, the author asked the director if he had a strategic plan for his prisons. The director's response was illustrative of reactive, as opposed to proactive, leadership. He stated that it was difficult being a "democrat" when the governor was a "republican," and that locking horns with the governor and his staff was a practical reality given the differing political allegiances. When the author suggested that "politics" could be taken out of the equation, and that the real question was one of effectively managing and leading the department of corrections, the director's response was that it was not the time to "confront" the governor. He added that the department had actually done well in the previous budgetary cycle, so there was no reason to "make waves" and further damage the fractured relationship that the department already had with the governor's office.

In short, the director in charge of the give-back program was not going to lead. Instead, he chose to react, even when he knew that such a posture would actually be more detrimental to his authority and leadership and to the operations of the state's prisons. In fact, when he finally left the position as director of the department of corrections, many correctional insiders suggested it was because he could not foster and forge more positive relationships with the governor's office and other key legislators who were critical of the amount of money the department was receiving in relation to other key public expenditures, such as education.

In a rather ironic way, during the 1990s when correctional budgets became a significant portion of the public budgets, correctional leaders kept silent on how these budgets should be spent, whether such spending was wise, and whether the increased spending actually provided some increases in public safety, offender rehabilitation, and victim assistance. At a time when correctional leaders should have been the most vocal and actually *leading,* many were simply silent, especially in relation to their governors or executives. As mentioned, this abdication has fostered many of the problems we now face in prisons as we begin the 21st century: too many prisoners, too few resources, conflicting purposes and aims, overworked staff, and a disgruntled and vociferous band of critics ready to castigate us for not exhibiting leadership qualities in addressing some of the most vexing and pressing problems that departments of corrections have ever had to face.

Establishing positive relationships with governors and other executives will have to become more relevant and important for correctional leaders of the future. For directors and secretaries of corrections and for prison leaders, this will mean more involvement at the political level with key executives and their representatives. In its final form, effective correctional leadership requires both a practical strategic plan as well as a political plan for how correctional leaders will function with political persons and groups. In the authors' experience as correctional consultants, prison officials and department of corrections personnel are too far removed from the political workings of governors' or executives' offices to be considered key players in how correctional matters will be addressed.

Legislatures.   A second political entity with which correctional leaders have to develop a more constructive relationship is the legislature. For most departments of corrections, the legislature is the most important group when it comes to correctional matters. Yet, many correctional leaders have not developed a plan of action on how to advance correctional interests with this group.

Note that it does not matter whether leaders are correctional executives or prison wardens. That is not an important distinction from a leadership perspective. Although this book has focused on prison leaders, leadership cuts across rank and functional lines, both within prisons and within the department of corrections. Wardens and their superiors within departments of corrections may not always be congruent concerning legislative strategy; but the point is that both groups should be more involved in the political processes to promote those issues and agendas that best reflect the mission and vision of the department of corrections.

Legislators are important actors who can either constructively or destructively affect correctional leadership, yet no two legislators have the same degree of influence in the political process. For correctional leadership to be effective, an initial assessment of *key* legislators has to be done. From this assessment, specific strategies or courses of action can be determined and pursued by correctional leaders. We agree with Garrett (1999) that prison administrators and managers need not be intricately involved in setting the public agenda for corrections. Instead, corrections officials, particularly correctional leaders, should play the role of the educator and inform significant legislators about the functioning of prisons. The words of Garrett (1999) are revelatory in this regard:

> The leaders of successful correctional agencies are those who are capable of cultivating the critical outside support necessary to deal with the individuals who are intent on wholesale change of the institution regimen. Outside support is necessary in the local, state, and national communities and is generally composed of the media, the judiciary, and the popularly elected legislative bodies. The image of corrections is very much in the hands of chief executive officers [or *leaders*, to use our word] of facilities and heads of correctional agencies. Effective leaders in these roles will gather support for their work by being responsive to their constituencies and bringing them inside to show them the realities of institutional responsibilities. (pp. 441–442)

Through a collaborative strategy with key legislators, correctional leaders can breathe life into their mission statements and visions. Without legislative support, the relationship between correctional leaders and the legislature will be potentially contentious, and possibly vitriolic. Too often correctional leaders interact with legislators with a "don't hurt me" posture or a confrontational strategy. On one occasion, a correctional administrator suggested that avoidance of troublesome legislators was the best strategy to protect corrections from legislative encroachment. Such a strategy, however, actually does more harm than good, since it does not allow correctional leaders to put their best foot forward and properly educate legislators about the issues and concerns they face when managing correctional institutions. Avoidance as a leadership strategy is an uninformed policy. Without proactive correctional leadership, the view and, ultimately, the direction of the legislature vis-à-vis the corrections department is determined to a large degree by anecdotes, images, perceptions, distortions, and even, in some cases, misrepresentations of others concerning correctional matters. This is a recipe for disaster for correctional leaders.

A more productive posture is one is which correctional leadership is more vocal and is present when the parameters of the correctional debate are being defined by the legislature. More often than not, the debate on how a department of corrections is to be viewed and supported (usually this means financial support) by a legislature is defined by the actions of a select few legislators. For this reason, effective correctional leadership needs a positive presence in the legislature and, most importantly, direct linkages with those key legislators who are either supportive or critical of the department. In the 21st century, prison leaders and the departments they work for will need direct relationships with legislators for effective leadership to be possible. Playing the "political game" is not the purpose of such relationships. Rather, the goal is to educate legislators about the issues and concerns that correctional leaders face, as well as informing them about the implications of intended legislation on correctional operations in clear and precise terms.

The education of legislators by correctional leaders is critical to correctional leadership and the functioning of prisons in the 21st century. If we learned anything about the relationship between legislators and correctional administrators during the latter part of the 20th century, it was that too often legislative changes in laws can produce significant and, in some cases, deleterious effects on the management and leadership of prisons. Legislative changes such as draconian "three-strikes-and-you're-out" laws during the 1990s produced a number of profound and damaging effects on the operations of prisons, and virtually no voices of reason responded to the state and federal governments that passed such laws. This has made both correctional management and correctional leadership difficult. Unless correctional leaders are willing to dialogue and inform the public discourse on prisons more directly, they will continue to suffer the consequences of poorly conceived laws that clearly produce more harm than good for all those involved in prisons, beginning with the prisoners but including correctional staff and those who manage and lead prisons.

Unions.   The third and final political entity we wish to address is the correctional union. Correctional unions across the United States are diverse, and on the political dimension, they have uneven power. In some states, correctional unions are extremely powerful groups, influencing public policy directly and being major players in executive-level politics. In most states, however, correctional unions are not influential; in many states, they have no political clout or influence with either the governor's office or the legislature. Correctional unions, for the most part, are small players in the political processes of state politics. Yet, this situation may change as we progress into the 21st century.

Correctional unions in prison are in a difficult position, as they serve both an internal and external constituent group. As an internal entity, correctional unions attend to the demands and interests of their members, representing workers on issues such as wages, benefits, and pensions. This is not an unusual position to be in for a union. What is atypical is that correctional unions if organized correctly are also an external constituent group, that represents the interests of the union within the political arena. As stated by Stojkovic and Lovell (1997), correctional leaders are significantly affected by the negotiations and relationships unions have outside the interests of the correctional staff and personnel they represent in the prison. For correctional unions, playing the political game is endemic to their struggle to develop and maintain the best bargaining position vis-à-vis the prison hierarchy. This means being more adroit in the political process and influencing both executive and legislative bodies, as well as other larger political interests, to advance their interests.

In one state where the authors work as consultants, the power of the correctional union is so influential that it is common to hear from correctional administrators how their bargaining advantage is limited and the operations of their facilities are extremely difficult due to the political connections the union president has with the governor's office and significant legislators. This particular correctional union was the second highest contributor to the coffers of two previous gubernatorial elections and is well connected to the legislature. One union official was so brash as to gloat that the governor was "our boy that we bought and paid for." For our purposes, however, the larger question is how political power was generated and sustained by that correctional union.

The acquisition of political power by correctional unions is not an overnight phenomenon. Significant political relationships are developed over years of doing battle and being frustrated with a correctional administration that is highly autocratic and indifferent to the needs of correctional employees. Powerful correctional unions do not ascend to the zenith of political power as a result of membership dues and the ability to financially support candidates. Rather, their political power is developed over many years of struggle with correctional systems that treat them poorly, overwork employees, pay modest wages, and do very little to assist employees in their own development and growth. Out of these conditions, some correctional unions have fared very well during the past 20 years on those matters that mean something to their members, such as wages, pensions, benefits, and, most importantly, input into how prisons are run.

Political power among correctional unions is, as stated earlier, not the same in every state. For most correctional unions, strong political influence is nonexistent *today*. Tomorrow is another day. We believe that in many states, correctional unions will become more politically astute. They will recognize that they have both internal and external obligations to their members, and if they want to do better in the political process, they will have to marshal political support external to the prison to advance their interests. In many states, the seeds for greater involvement by correctional unions in the legislative and gubernatorial processes of the states have been planted by the past practices of correctional administrators. This will bear fruit for correctional unions, and they will be a formidable foe in both the organizational context of the prison and the political arena where all correctional matters are defined and implemented.

As stated earlier, correctional unions are not the problem; the real problem is in how correctional leaders respond to them. How correctional leaders respond to the growing political power of correctional unions will define, in part, how effective these leaders will become in the 21st century. Effective correctional leadership will mean developing and defining the leader's relationship to correctional unions. These unions will not go away. If anything they will become more permanently ensconced on the correctional landscape, and as with governors and legislators, they will be important entities for correctional leaders to address in the future.

Policy and Research Considerations

The nexus between policy and research has always been tenuous in corrections. For practical-minded correctional leaders, the value of research is problematic. In an excellent piece that highlights the connections between research and policy, Lovell (1988) documents how one department of corrections used research in the policy development process. According to Lovell, research was most likely to be used by correctional administrators in a *conceptual* way, that is, holding the view that research is important but not providing any specificity as to how and when research findings can be employed to create policy. Another way research was used, according to Lovell, was in a *symbolic* way. Here research is viewed as a tool to get budgets passed or to garner some support for a program or initiative without any real connection between a specific piece of research and a particular policy choice. A final way research was used by correctional administrators was in an *instrumental* way. This describes the use of research to directly affect policy. According to Lovell, this type of research is the least common and least used by correctional administrators, since policy and research are rarely connected at all in the world of corrections.

Research can have a significant role in helping to frame debates on policy issues. It can offer assistance in the allocation of scarce resources directed toward programming efforts and provide some guidance to correctional administrators concerning the efficacy of programming efforts offered in the prison setting. Yet, the nexus between policy and research will, in the foreseeable future, remain ambiguous and difficult for correctional leaders for two reasons. First, the world of corrections is inherently a political world where values and preferences dominate. In such a world, the factual revelations of social science research are often irrelevant. For example, research that shows the limited and narrow value of such correctional practices as boot camps and chain gangs to crime reduction may have little effect on such programmatic choices, which often are part of the political agendas of influential parties in the political process. In the long sordid history of correctional reform, empirical facts have been a poor defense to the onslaught of political preferences of the day.

Research has often been understood as a luxury, and not a necessity, in making choices concerning correctional policies.

The second reason the policy-research nexus is likely to remain difficult for correctional leaders is that the world of social science research is not the world of the correctional professional. Social scientists talk about averages and measures of central tendency; they are interested in the most typical outcome. Correctional professionals, on the other hand, live in an atypical world, one where that which is unusual is relevant. For example, a sex offender who violates his conditions of parole and kills someone is of importance to them. The reverberations of such an event mean something to correctional professionals and the public. In the political world of corrections, attempting to deal with the horrific atypical case is what defines correctional leadership, even though in many instances correctional leaders are powerless to address these unusual events. Yet, providing the *appearance* of being a problem solver is the essence of correctional leadership in the eyes of a critical and unforgiving public.

How are we to reconcile the differences between these two worlds? We do have some examples in our correctional history where particular correctional leaders were influenced by, and able to influence significant others about, the importance of correctional research to correctional policy. One such person was Richard McGee in the state of California from 1944 to 1961. We mentioned earlier the contributions of McGee to the discussion of correctional leadership. What significantly separated McGee as a correctional leader from both his predecessors and successors was his insistence on good research informing correctional policy.

Glaser (1995), in his outstanding book on the career of Richard McGee, documents how research played a pivotal role in McGee's tenure as director of the California Department of Corrections. McGee was fervent about how research should inform policy choices and demanded from his staff the empirical bases for the decisions they made. He hired new students in the field of social science research in the 1960s to develop and implement a social science regimen to guide decision making in the department of corrections. Glaser produced his seminal work, *The Effectiveness of a Prison and Parole System* (1964), while working in the California Department of Corrections. Other significant reports and research findings, such as those by Don Gottfredson, Norman Holt, and John Conrad, were also products of McGee's insistence on and support for a research-based policy decision-making process. In McGee's world, corrections had to be informed by research in order to have a positive impact on prisons and prisoners.

Prior to his departure from the California Department of Corrections, McGee gave to the incoming governor, Ronald Reagan, his ideas, thoughts, and recommendations for corrections and even offered a series of predictions about where corrections was heading. Unfortunately, according to Glaser (1995), it is not clear whether Governor Reagan ever read McGee's report. What we do know is that McGee's hope that social science research would guide correctional policy was doomed to failure given the series of political, social, and economic changes in both the state of California and the United States from the mid-1960s to the end of the 20th century.

In spite of this ending, McGee's ideas on the connection between research and policy development have been revived by many concerned about correctional matters, especially correctional leaders. It is not uncommon for both researchers and policy makers in numerous public settings to work together to address questions concerning both outputs and outcomes regarding programming efforts. More and more we are seeing public agencies pursuing ongoing research initiatives to evaluate the effectiveness of their programs. In a wide variety of criminal justice settings, research has become more than a luxury item shuffled to the bottom of organizational priority lists when resources are tight. Instead, we are seeing a greater reliance on systematically collected and analyzed data in arriving at decisions.

While correctional organizations will always be "political" in how they use and interpret research findings, many are recognizing and valuing the nexus between research and policy making. The "garbage can" model of organizational decision making is slowly being replaced by a "well of knowledge" model predicated on research. Priorities and preferences are gradually being realigned so that research and correctional policy making are brought together to assist correctional leaders in effectively accomplishing their missions.

CORRECTIONAL LEADERSHIP: SCENARIOS AND CONCLUDING COMMENTS

We envision three possible scenarios for correctional leadership in the 21st century. The first we call the "business as usual" scenario. In this scenario, correctional leaders continue to perform in a traditional way. By this we mean that their procedures, practices, and policies mirror what they have always done: They continue to be reactive in addressing correctional problems, controlled by the political and social vagaries of the day, and show little concern for the "future," responding to issues and concerns in a bureaucratic way with little hope for change.

We believe the business-as-usual scenario will not be able to address the pressing problems that correctional leaders will face in this century, including prison overcrowding, a world of infinite expectations constrained by limited resources, challenges to correctional leadership by "private" entrepreneurs who view the correctional landscape as fertile ground for making profits, a shrinking and less prepared workforce where correctional labor shortages will become the norm, and an ever-restless public that will demand more concrete results for the dollars they are spending on correctional ventures. Employing traditional ways of leading and managing prisons will not be able to address this confluence of factors that will make correctional work even more difficult in the future than it is now.

Another possible scenario for the future of correctional leadership is what we term the "correctional-crisis" scenario. In this scenario, the prison is viewed as getting worse than it is now. Prison overcrowding becomes more intractable; health care and the management of health care issues become more problematic as correctional health care dollars are not available to meet the prisoner demand; correctional employees become more difficult to recruit and, more importantly, to retain, and turnover among prison staff is high and difficult to manage for prison officials; and finally correctional leaders do not last. The incentives for being a prison manager or leader are reduced, and the problems too onerous to handle. Younger and inexperienced persons are moved quickly into administrative positions without the requisite training and experience so prison problems become even more difficult to handle effectively. Correctional leadership is defined by the ability to jump and manage burgeoning and nascent correctional problems, forcing correctional leaders to operate in a deficiency mode from crisis to crisis. Crisis management, not leadership, becomes the typical way of addressing prison problems. Another common feature of this scenario is the micromanagement of the prison by higher officials in the department of corrections and even politicians' and governors' offices.

The final scenario is what we term the "optimistic" scenario. In this scenario, correctional leaders emerge. Departments of corrections invest in the future by supporting strategic planning and the development of correctional leaders. Leaders are cultivated in the department along a career ladder arrangement. Emphasis is on defining more precisely the correctional mission and vision for the department and the prisons. Challenges and problems abound, yet there is a belief among correctional employees, managers, and leaders that something can be done to address these problems and issues. Correctional leaders are optimistic, energetic, and passionate about their work. They lead by example; they encourage others beneath them to grow in their positions within the prison. These leaders not only establish a purpose for the prison, but they also show through their behavior that their words can be believed.

Most importantly, correctional leaders in our optimistic scenario are passionate about their work. They recognize that correctional leadership does not reside in a position, but is found in a mind-set and a commitment to something that is valued by correctional employees. Moreover, they recognize that correctional leadership is a process that must be buttressed by a conviction that correctional work is important and that employees are the lifeblood of the organization. As one correctional official in the country of South Africa relayed to one of the authors, "Corrections work is people work. Without good people, we cannot sustain the prison, nor can we assist prisoners in any meaningful way." At the core of correctional leadership is how much leaders invest in the cultures they engender within their prisons.

We finish this book where we began: Effective correctional leadership is about the creation, perpetuation, and sustainment of a positive correctional culture within the prison. This culture is an amalgamation of many cultures; we identified and discussed the three primary cultures found within prisons. The main challenge for correctional leadership is to make a conscious effort to work and align these three cultures around a central mission and vision for the prison. Although prisons vary on many dimensions, effective correctional leadership for the 21st century means a commitment to the ideas and expressions exhibited within the final "optimistic" scenario. The "business-as-usual" and "correctional-crisis" scenarios have run their courses and should be left to the dustbins of 20th century correctional history. Effective correctional leadership of the 21st century requires optimism, a correctional vision that recognizes people as the core of correctional work, and the development of a positive correctional culture within the prison. This is the essence of correctional leadership.

CASE SCENARIO   *Correctional Leadership and Politics*

The executive leadership within the department of corrections had been in a constant state of flux. The state had been unable to maintain stable leadership within the executive ranks of the department of corrections due, in part, to the perception among correctional officials that power politics defined the governor's choice of persons to lead the department. Because of this perception, many good and qualified correctional personnel had put out the word that they were not interested in the department's top position. Instead, they viewed themselves as career service personnel waiting until the time and dollars were right to retire. In the language of the department, these seasoned correctional officials were waiting for the proverbial "golden handshake."

This perception fueled the already antagonistic relationship that had existed for two decades between the correctional leadership and the correctional officer union. The union had been politically active; it had successfully negotiated collective bargaining agreements with the state that were generous and financially advantageous to correctional officers, while at the same time contributing major dollars to the coffers of elected officials who supported its positions. The department of corrections felt powerless in negotiating with the union, since in the words of a former director of the department, the governor was "in bed with the union." In fact, it was common knowledge that the union had contributed a significant amount of money to the current governor's initial election and reelection campaigns. In return, the union had received major concessions and a very good labor contract from the state.

Correctional leaders within the department felt powerless to act. For many of them, politics was a dirty word. While they recognized that being part of the political process was essential and endemic to correctional leadership, they had no clue on how to proceed in this process. Moreover, many correctional leaders viewed the political strategies of the union to be unethical and immoral. Because they were state employees, they were precluded from doing things that the union could do, such as donating money to political campaigns. But their political problems went deeper than the internal politics of the department.

The leaders in the department often acted in a shortsighted fashion, reacting rather than proactively taking their views and ideas to the governor's office and the legislature. Additionally, they lived in constant fear: fear of the governor, fear of the legislature, fear of the media, and fear of the courts. These fears paralyzed the department; the leaders could never act, at least act in time, to respond to issues and events. Through micromanagement and traditionally defined bureaucratic procedures, the department limped along, lacking any sense of purpose, direction, and mission. In fact, by not leading, departmental officials became more susceptible to control and review by those they feared the most: the governor and his staff. Due to the lack of leadership in the department, the governor and others were using the department for their pet political projects and narrowly defined agendas. The central questions for correctional leaders were: Who was really leading

Case Scenario continued

the department of corrections? What was the proper relationship between correctional leaders and political figures?

Case Scenario Questions

1. What balance should exist between correctional leaders and politicians and political groups? What are the competing concerns among these groups, and why are they relevant to effective correctional leadership?

2. What are the consequences of viewing a correctional union as "the problem" in the political process? Do union and correctional leader relations have to be strained? Suggest a proactive approach to dealing with correctional unions.

3. Why is fear a crippling factor for correctional leadership? Discuss the effects of being afraid to lead within correctional organizations. Describe positive ways that fear can be addressed by correctional leaders.

REFERENCES

Banner, D. K., & Gagne, T. E. (1995). *Designing effective organizations*. Thousand Oaks, CA: Sage.

Bass, B. M., & Avolio, B. J. (1994). *Improving organizational effectiveness through transformational leadership*. Thousand Oaks, CA: Sage.

Beck, A. J., & Karberg, J. C. (2001). Prison and jail inmates at midyear 2000. U.S. Department of Justice: Bureau of Justice Statistics.

Bond, M. A., & Pyle, J. L. (1998). The ecology of diversity in organizational settings: Lessons from a case study. *Human Relations, 51*(5), 589–623.

Bureau of Labor Statistics. (2000). Occupational outlook handbook: Correctional officer. Available: http://stats.bls.gov/oco/ocos156.htm.

Cullen, F. T., Link, B. G., Wolfe, N. T., & Frank, J. (1985). The social dimensions of correctional officer stress. *Justice Quarterly, 2*(4), 505–533.

Evlon, D., & Bamberger, P. (2000). Empowerment cognitions and empowerment acts: Recognizing the importance of gender. *Group and organization management, 25*(4): 354–372.

Fullerton, H. N. (1999, November). Labor force projections to 2008: Steady growth and changing composition. *Monthly Labor Review,* 19–32.

Garrett, J. S. (1999). Political involvement in penal operations. In P. M. Carlson & J. S. Garrett (Eds.), *Prison and jail administration: Practice and theory* (pp. 438–442). Gaithersburg, MD: Aspen.

Gilbert, M. J. (1999). The illusion of structure: A critique of the classical model of organization and the discretionary power of correctional officers. In S. Stojkovic, J. Klofas, & D. Kalinich (Eds.), *The administration and management of criminal justice organizations: A book of readings* (3rd ed., pp. 263–277). Prospect Heights, IL: Waveland.

Glaser, D. (1964). *The effectiveness of a prison and parole system*. Indianapolis, IN: Bobbs-Merrill.

Glaser, D. (1995). *Preparing convicts for law-abiding lives: The pioneering penology of Richard A. McGee.* Albany, NY: State University of New York Press.

Henderson, G. (1994). *Cultural diversity in the workplace.* Westport, CT: Quorum Books.

Herenkohl, R. C., Judson, G. T., & Heffner, J. A. (1999). Defining and measuring employee empowerment. *The Journal of Applied Behavioral Science, 35*(3), 373–389.

Jurik, N., & Winn, R. (1987). Describing correctional security dropouts and rejects: An individual or organizational profile? *Criminal Justice and Behavior, 14*(1), 5–25.

Kiekbusch, R. G. (2001). The looming correctional work force shortage: A problem of supply and demand. *Corrections Compendium, 26*(4), 1–3, 24–25.

Koberg, C. S., Boss, R. W., Senjem, J. C., & Goodman, E. A. (1999). Antecedents and outcomes of empowerment. *Group and Organization Management, 24*(1): 71–91.

Lindquist, C., & Whitehead, J. (1986). Burnout, job stress, and job satisfaction among southern correctional officers: Perceptions and causal factors. *Journal of Offender Counseling, Services, and Rehabilitation, 10*(4), 5–25.

Loden, M., & Rosener, J. B. (1991). *Workforce America! Managing employee diversity as a vital resource.* Homewood, IL: Business One Irwin.

Lombardo, L. X. (1981). Occupational stress in correctional officers: Sources, coping strategies, and implications. In S. E. Zimmerman & H. D. Miller (Eds.), *Corrections at the crossroads* (pp. 129–149). Beverly Hills, CA: Sage.

Lovell, R. (1988). Research utilization on complex organizations: A case study in corrections. *Justice Quarterly, 5*(2), 257–280.

Patenaude, A. L. (2001). Analysis of issues affecting correctional officer retention within the Arkansas Department of Corrections. *Corrections Management Quarterly, 5*(2), 49–67.

Patterson, B. L. (1992). Job experience and perceived job stress among police, correctional and probation/parole officers. *Criminal Justice and Behavior, 19*(3), 260–285.

Pogrebin, M., & Atkins, B. (1982). Organizational conflict in correctional institutions. *Journal of Offender Counseling, Services, and Rehabilitation, 7*(1), 23–31.

Rainey, H. G. (1997). *Understanding and managing public organizations.* San Francisco: Jossey-Bass.

Schein, E. H. (1992). *Organizational culture and leadership.* San Francisco: Jossey-Bass.

Silverman, I. J. (2001). *Corrections: A comprehensive view.* Belmont, CA: West/Wadsworth.

Stojkovic, S., Kalinich, D., & Klofas, J. (1998). *Criminal justice organizations administration and management* (2nd ed.). Belmont, CA: West/Wadsworth.

Stojkovic, S., & Lovell, R. (1997). *Corrections: An introduction* (2nd ed.). Cincinnati, OH: Anderson.

Stupak, R. (1999). Creating the future: Strategic positioning in corrections. In P. M. Carlson & J. S. Garrett (Eds.), *Prison and jail administration: Practice and theory* (pp. 443–450). Gaithersburg, MD: Aspen.

INDEX